This HOUSE is NUTS!

This HOUSE is NUTS!

Linwood Barclay

Illustrations by Steve Nease

Published in 1997 by Stoddart Publishing Co. Limited
34 Lesmill Road, Toronto, Canada M3B 2T6

Distributed in Canada by General Distribution Services Limited
34 Lesmill Road, Toronto, Canada M3B 2T6
Tel. (416) 445-3333 Fax (416) 445-5967
E-mail Customer.Service@ccmailgw.genpub.com

Distributed in the U.S. by General Distribution Services Inc.
85 River Rock Drive, Suite 202, Buffalo, New York 14207
Toll-free tel. 1-800-805-1083 Toll-free fax 1-800-481-6207
E-mail gdsinc@genpub.com

01 00 99 98 97   1 2 3 4 5

Cataloguing in Publication Data

Barclay, Linwood
This house is nuts

ISBN 0-7737-3056-7

1. Family - Humor.   I. Title
PS8553.A7433T44 1997   C818'.5402   97-931930-7
PR9199.3.B37T44 1997

Text design: Tannice Goddard
Computer layout: Mary Bowness

Printed and bound in Canada

We gratefully acknowledge the Canada Council for the Arts and the Ontario Arts Council for their support of our publishing program.

For Neetha, Spencer, and Paige.
Like, who else?

Contents

Introduction:
Welcome to Our Nutty Home

When did we first realize our house was nuts?

If I were asked to provide a date, I would choose December 21, 1986, seventeen days after the birth of our daughter Paige.

My wife Neetha was downstairs, preparing something on the stove. I had taken Paige, whom I was able to carry in the crook of my arm like a football, her head resting in my palm, upstairs to be changed.

I had set her on her back, her legs kicking about furiously, on the change table in her bedroom, and was just undoing the diaper when my son Spencer, a couple of months away from his third birthday, poked his head around the door.

He was standing at the foot of the change table, his eyes level with it, and was watching these proceedings with considerable interest, at least until the contents of said diaper became visible.

It was, I have to admit, not a pretty sight. But as a parent, you develop some immunity to these kinds of spectacles. You become strong. You become stoic. You hold your breath.

But Spencer had developed none of these characteristics. He had, however, mastered a terrific dry-heaving technique.

His face went pale and he started sending out all the signals that he was about to lose his lunch.

I had what you might call a dilemma.

On the one hand, I had a seventeen-day-old National Ballet hopeful who wanted to tap her feet into the grossest mess imaginable, and on the other, an extremely queasy small boy with dubious career prospects as a pediatrician and a dire need to be guided to a toilet.

I did what any smart husband would do. I screamed for my wife.

"Neetha!"

Paige was too small to be able to roll over, so I briefly left her to run Spencer across the hall into the bathroom. "Come on, come on!" I said to him.

I stood him in front of the toilet and flung up the seat with such force that when it hit the tank it bounced back, landing right on Spencer's head.

"Whaaaaaa!"

At least it took his mind off his sick stomach.

Meanwhile, I could hear Neetha racing up the stairs. "Check on Paige!" I shouted from the bathroom. From Paige's room I could hear Neetha say: "Yuck! What have you DONE to your FEET?"

While I calmed Spencer and kissed the bump on his head, Neetha got Paige cleaned up, into a new diaper, and tucked into her crib. A couple of moments later, we met in the hall. I told her what had happened.

As we leaned into each other for support, I sniffed the air. "Is, uh, something burning?"

"Oh god!" Neetha shrieked and charged back down to the kitchen.

So we were now a complete family, with a son and a daughter, and well on our way to becoming completely nuts.

Some years have passed since then, and there have been a lot of changes, not the least of which is that in 1993, I began to record our domestic adventures for *The Toronto Star*, where, for more than twelve years, I'd been an editor. The family may not have always liked the hours I worked as an assistant city editor, or news editor, or Life section editor, but at least their daily escapades remained a secret from millions of readers. The stories in the chapters that follow chronicle our lives from then to now, during which time Spencer went from the age of nine to thirteen, and Paige from six to ten.

For all this time I've felt rather confident that my columns have provided an accurate account of our lives, but one recent incident did give me pause.

You see, our friend Leslie was in a bookstore in Owen Sound, Ontario, when she spotted my first book, *Father Knows Zilch: A Guide for Dumbfounded Dads*, on the shelf. She showed my photo on the back cover to her young daughter Sarah and infant son Jack and said: "Look, there's Spencer's and Paige's daddy."

A woman standing next to her turned and said, "Your kids actually KNOW Spencer and Paige? I read about them all the time in the paper in that man's column, and I always thought they were fictional."

I laughed when I first heard this story, but the more I thought about it, the more worried I became. Was it possible? Could it be that my two children, and by extension, Neetha, were merely figments of my imagination? Was I more nuts than our house? Could it be that these people I lived with, day in and day out, did not, technically speaking, exist?

When you begin to suspect that the people you love may not be real, some pretty big, cosmic-type questions come to mind, like: How will this affect my book contract?

If the house isn't real, do I have to give back the advance?

And if it turns out that I, too, am fictional, am I in trouble for cashing the cheque?

It would be a shame to find out my family is not real because I've grown quite attached to them. So I drew up a short test, "How to Know Whether You and Your Family Truly Exist," which I felt would help me determine whether my loved ones were authentic. (Feel free to take it yourself if you're having any doubts about your own family.)

- Do most of the funny things that happen in your family take about thirty minutes to run their course, and is there a moral at the end?
- Are your kids precocious way beyond their years, and do they always get off the best lines?
- Do you sometimes hear great hoots of laughter but can't tell where they're coming from?
- Do you have a wacky neighbour who always comes into your house without knocking?

- Unlike other people on your street, who are worried about their mortgage, is your family consumed with fears of cancellation?
- Is the father in your household all-knowing and wise?

If the answer to these questions is Yes, you have reason to be concerned. You are living in a sitcom. But I'm relieved to report that I answered No to every question, particularly that last one. As the following chapters will show, it's rare that anyone under this roof views me in that light.

So welcome to life with the Barclays, and make yourself at home. Chances are you'll agree our house is nuts. The question is, is it as nuts as yours?

Recipes for Disaster

The Kitchen

Just *make* a decision

"What will we have for dinner tonight?"

This is an oft-asked question in the morning at our place. Just as we're clearing away the breakfast dishes and preparing to head off on our separate ways, Neetha will look in the freezer.

"What about chicken?" she asks. "If we're going to have chicken, I'll take it out now and put it in the fridge to thaw."

I haven't said anything yet. I'm looking at the bowl of shredded wheat Paige has just left on the counter top. She is leaving the kitchen, saying she is full, and has left in her bowl what looks like a milk-soaked condor's nest.

"Did you eat ANY of this?" I ask her.

"Yes!"

"This looks like the exact same amount as I gave you."

"I'm full!"

"What about spaghetti?"

"Hmmm?"

"Spaghetti. That'll be fast. Let's have spaghetti tonight."

"Okay, spaghetti."

But Neetha is still looking in the freezer. I thought things had been settled. "I'll need to thaw some meat if you want to have a meat sauce. Do you just want tomato sauce or do you want meat?"

"Uhh, I don't care," I say. "Do whatever you want."

At which point Neetha gives me one of those looks. When you've been married as long as we have you know when you're getting one of those looks. If you've been married this long and DON'T know when you're getting one of those looks, you should start getting your affairs in order. Your days are numbered.

Neetha doesn't actually say anything, but if she were going to, it would be this:

"First, I looked in the cupboards and fridge and figured out what we needed. Then I made a list. Then I figured out what would be some good things to have for dinner for the next week, and planned five days' worth of menus. Then I headed over to the grocery store with two kids trying to kill each other who kept asking over and over and over again whether they could have fourteen boxes of Pizza Pops.

"I wandered up and down the aisles with one of those carts where the wheel's wobbling so badly you think you're on a Nicaraguan bus tour, and got everything we needed in this house to keep us alive. Then I went to the checkout, getting behind a woman who paid by cheque and had to present twenty-three pieces of identification plus bring in two character witnesses, and still she questioned the cashier about the price of her Double Stuf Oreos, accusing her of ringing it in wrong.

"When I took back the shopping cart it wouldn't return my quarter.

"Then I brought everything home, dragged it into the house, and put it all away. And now, NOW, all I'm asking from YOU is to tell me: Do you want a regular tomato sauce, or DO YOU WANT MEAT?"

But the thing is, I really don't know. I can go either way on this. I like a regular tomato sauce, but on the other hand, a sauce with some meat in it, well, that's good, too.

What if I say I want a meat sauce, and Neetha defrosts the meat, and then when dinnertime comes, I wish I'd opted for just sauce? What about that? These are the kinds of things that worry me.

But as I said, there is something in Neetha's expression that tells me a decision must be made. It doesn't have to be the right decision, it just has to be any decision.

"Well," I say, "a meat sauce would be nice."

"So you do want a meat sauce?"

"Yes," I say with conviction. "I want a meat sauce. Never in my life have I felt more strongly about something than I do right now about meat sauce."

"Okay, I'll thaw some meat."

"Great. Unless you want regular sauce, which is fine by me, since I like that just as well."

If you know someone who could assist me with getting my affairs in order, please drop me a line.

Reading this over breakfast? Sit down

If it's Saturday, there's a good chance I'm sitting down to breakfast. This is a bigger deal than it might sound.

That's because, through the week, while I do find time to eat breakfast, I never do so in a sitting position.

There are two kinds of people in the world: those who sit down to eat their breakfast and those who accomplish it standing up. Neetha falls into the first category. I find myself in the latter. I know what you're wondering. Can this marriage be saved?

While Neetha would prefer I sat down to eat breakfast, she doesn't make an issue of it Monday through Friday. She has bigger things to worry about, such as trying to do up the temperamental zipper on her new coat, which never takes less than five minutes.

But if I'm on my feet with a bowl of cereal in my hand on the weekend, I'm in trouble. Often, as a kind of preemptive strike, Neetha will make us coffee. She knows I can't drink coffee and stand up at the same time. Toast is toast, but coffee is sacred.

I'd like to think that things are just so busy for us in the morning — getting ourselves ready for the day, getting Spencer and Paige up for school, pulling together the lunches, hauling out the snowsuits — that there's no time for sitting.

But that won't wash with Neetha who, despite having to be out the door by 7:40, believes you must sit for breakfast, even if it's nothing more than buttered toast. I wouldn't touch my bottom to chair for toast if my daybook were clear right through till Christmas.

(Neetha tells me she even sits for breakfast when she's alone. I'd eat a seven-course meal standing up if I were alone. Over the sink.)

For Neetha, these are precious moments, possibly the only chance she gets all day to sit in peace. Sitting for breakfast, in the lean and mean '90s, is what passes for spoiling yourself.

At least as a member of the eat-standing club, I'm not alone. Millions of people eat breakfast on their feet, particularly those eating on the run. You see them at the muffin stands by the subways, or standing at the bus stop, warming themselves with a take-out cup of coffee.

One way to be sure you can sit down for breakfast is to take it to the office with you. There you can settle in behind your desk, open up your brown Tim Horton's bag and, between bites of apple fritter, review all the work that stretches before you.

But if sitting for breakfast means you're already working, well, Neetha probably wouldn't see that as an improvement over standing.

Perhaps I'm setting a poor example for Spencer and Paige.

Once I've gently nudged them from under their covers in the direction of the breakfast table by going into their rooms and turning on their CD players at full volume, they take their seats in the kitchen, where I can admire hairbumps that rank with the pyramids as masterpieces of engineering.

It's while preparing their breakfasts that I consume my own. I have this timed out perfectly. I can, for example, eat most of a bowl of Cheerios in the time it takes to do Spencer's toast. Half a banana can be consumed while warming milk in the microwave for Paige's shredded wheat. A glass of juice can be downed while rummaging in the drawer for spoons. And you can't load a dishwasher between orange wedges or turn up Valerie Pringle's interview with some brain-dead Hollywood star who's going on about how his film works on several levels, if you're glued to a chair.

This is what's known in the '90s as multi-tasking. But sometimes breakfast is so busy, I have to sit down afterwards for a rest.

Forget Minute Rice. We have Minute Dinner

It's not just breakfast that's a blur at our house. Dinner can be equally hurried, especially during the summer, when we have what we call The Forty-Five-Second Dinner Hour.

It is 6 p.m., and Neetha and I are attempting to round up Spencer and Paige to come in for fuel. They've been playing all day with their friends from across the street, running in and out, making a haunted house in the basement out of chairs and thick flannel sheets, jumping through sprinklers, building Lego, and setting up tables at the end of the driveway in a bid to sell unwanted comics and trading cards.

They've repeatedly shouted "CARDS FOR SALE!" at the top of their lungs to an otherwise completely empty street, hopped on their bikes to ride around the block in a futile attempt to drum up business, and trashed the garage after their father told them for the forty-third time since lunch that he just cleaned the place up and could they leave it that way, please.

The chicken wings, corn on the cob, and sliced tomatoes are ready to be served. I call for them to come in.

The two bounce into the kitchen, their feet slapping against the floor. We, stupid parents that we are, have failed to co-ordinate dining times with the parents of their friends. This means that now *their* kids are idle, and once *ours* are let loose, *their* friends will be called in for supper, thereby idling *our* children. It would be easier to launch an invasion on Iraq.

Paige looks at the table. There is no food there. It's on the plates, which are on the counter, and which now must be moved a distance of five feet to the placemats.

"Dinner's not ready!" she says breathlessly. "I'm going to go back out and play some more!"

"Hold it!" we say. "Hold it right there!"

The plates make it to the table. So does the steaming hot corn.

We sit down and they dig into the chicken wings. Spencer has adopted the typical youngster's dining stance, which consists of one leg planted straight down on the floor, other leg bent, knee resting on the seat of the chair. He looks ready to shoot out of the starting blocks.

"Sit down properly."

Paige is still panting from tearing around outside. "We have to hurry," she says. "I have to find something to make into a communicator that I can stick on my arm. We're Predators."

We offer them some corn. They love corn.

"No thanks."

"No thanks."

Eating a cob of corn is too time-intensive even to be considered. "Eat," we say, our voices low like we really mean it, "some corn."

Reluctantly, they each reach for a buttered cob. The chicken wings are inhaled. With some relief, I notice that the bones are left on their plates. Spencer consumes at least three kernels of corn and asks, "May I be excused from the table?"

"May I be excused, too?" Paige asks.

We point out to them that their milk glasses are full. They pour the milk straight down their throats. It's a wonder they don't drown.

"This is all there's going to be," we warn them. "THIS is dinner. Don't come back in two hours saying you're hungry."

This is, of course, Empty Threat Number Twenty-Seven. As if, when they come in at nine, starving, we will deny them a snack so we can have the pleasure of being kept awake until 2 a.m. by the sounds of growling stomachs.

They plead with us that they are full. "Now?" they ask. "Can we PLEASE be excused NOW?"

We give them their freedom. We can hardly wait for the order that will be imposed by a return to school and homework. That's when we'll settle into The Fifty-Eight-Second Dinner Hour. Things take a little longer because once they're into long pants and shoes, there's more wind resistance.

We need an entry-level bagel toaster

We're having a coffee, waiting for the kids to conclude their business in a nearby bookstore, when Neetha says: "Here's a good idea for a column. Entry-level."

"Say again?"

"Entry-level. You know, it used to be, if you wanted something inexpensive, it was called the cheap model, but now it's called entry-level. Or how they try to get you to buy a more expensive item, and still call IT the entry-level model."

She offers as an example our experience earlier in the day when we were buying Paige's first pair of in-line skates. We explained to the salesperson that Paige, at age nine, was just starting out, so she didn't need the most sophisticated skates in the world, just some decent ones.

"Well," he said, "here's a good entry-level skate." And he showed us some fancy footwear with what appeared to be flying buttresses that constituted the newest, most advanced braking system, and all we would have to do is skip a couple of mortgage payments to afford them.

"What about these ones," I asked, "that cost about $65?"

"Oh sure, those are good."

But what I suspect Neetha's really doing by suggesting *this* column idea is to make me forget one that presented itself at breakfast. This would be a piece about Neetha trying to cover her tracks with peanut butter.

First, I have to offer some more breakfast background, and explain our bagel code of ethics. Bagels fresh from the bakery are *never* toasted. If they have that slightly squishy texture, that still-hot-from-the-oven feel to them, it seems wrong, no, it seems *criminal*, to toast them. Just cut them in half, spread on the cream cheese, and enjoy.

But a second-day bagel, a bagel that's not quite as soft as it was the day before, almost always ends up toasted, although this does not mean putting it into the toaster, but under the broiler in the oven. A split bagel will not fit in the toaster. Well, it might fit in the toaster, but you'd never get it back out, and at our house, you don't let your spouse poke around in a plugged-in toaster with a metal fork, unless of course said spouse is overinsured.

On this particular day, we are dealing with day-old bagels, so they're going to be run under the broiler. Neetha volunteers for this project if I'll set us up a place to eat outside and put on the kettle. "What do you want on your bagel?" she asks.

"Peanut butter, please," I say.

Neetha gives the broiler time to heat up, then puts the bagels on a metal tray, which she slides into the oven. Then she does a few other things, like get down some plates, put away a few glasses from the dishwasher, pour us some juice. In other words, enough things to make her forget that she has slid some bagels under the broiler.

Anyway, something finally clicks, and suddenly she's flinging open the oven door, throwing bagels onto plates, and slathering peanut butter onto mine like she's spackling a pie-sized hole in the wall. I peer over her shoulder.

"Do you figure if you put on enough peanut butter," I say, "I won't notice the bagel was briefly in flames?"

"After all these years," she says, "you're starting to know me too well."

Now, over our coffees, Neetha says: "And remember when we were looking at TVs, and there was this perfectly acceptable one, and they called it an entry-level TV because it didn't have some gizmo like a screen within a screen within a screen, which we would never use anyway?"

She's right. This "entry-level" thing is a good topic. I'm not going to bother with the bagel story after all.

The under-the-sink garbage game

Welcome to Family Corner!

This week, as part of Family Togetherness Week ("If You've Got to

The Kitchen

Live in a Family, It Might as Well Be Your Own!"), we're going to tell you about a terrific game that involves everyone, and can be played in your very own kitchen!

Patterned after "House of Cards," in which you delicately balance playing cards atop each other until they finally collapse, this new game requires skill, patience, and a knack for avoiding basic household responsibilities.

You're probably already playing this game at home and don't even realize it. We call it "Don't Topple the Trash!" and the rules are so simple you won't even have to write them down.

You know that garbage receptacle everyone has behind the cabinet door, right under the kitchen sink? Well, whenever you go to put something in that receptacle, you must ensure it stays there. You may already find this container spilling over with garbage. Pay no attention. Squeeze your trash in with it.

You must jam it in. You must force it in. Do whatever it takes if you want to win, even if that means balancing the trash on top and closing the door slowly so the wind currents don't knock it off.

This is the object of "Don't Topple the Trash!" The under-the-sink trash may already be overflowing with potato peelings. It may appear ready to explode with the fermenting half domes of ravaged grapefruit rinds. But as long as you're able to close that kitchen cabinet and walk away without hearing something fall over and spill its contents onto the Ajax, refundable bottles that should have been turned in months ago, and bottles of dishwashing liquid, you're still in the game.

The poor, miserable sap who comes along and, no matter how hard he tries, cannot get the garbage container to accept his contribution without it spilling out, and is forced to empty everything out into the can in the garage, is the loser.

I'm ashamed to have to tell you this, but I never win this game at our house. I am up against talented individuals who play for keeps. Neetha, Spencer, and Paige have what it takes to advance to the national championships.

If only I were sharp enough to follow these tips that can give you the advantage and drive your opponent nuts:

- When the receptacle's only half full, put in an empty waxed-cardboard milk container. (Orange juice containers will also work here.) Make no attempt to crush it. Milk cartons are terrific because they consume large amounts of space even though they weigh next to nothing. The next person to come along will attempt to squash the container to fit in his own trash, but chances are good the carton will spring back, thereby forcing the new garbage out. If you really want to play dirty, sneak in one of those clear, rigid plastic, croissant containers. One product research company found that not even a herd of elephants could flatten one of these suckers.
- If the trash is too full to accommodate the empty milk carton, just put it back in the fridge. So long as your household does not possess a Family Fingerprinting Kit, you can always blame someone else.
- When garbage is already teetering on the brink, discreetly take your trash someplace else in the house. Imagine the hilarity when someone finds banana peels and a container of sour cream from the Trudeau years in the master bedroom waste basket.

So there you have it! Next week, we'll give you some secret game-winning techniques for "Who'll Finally Take the New Box of Tide, Which Has Been Sitting at the Top of the Stair Here Since Last Weekend, Down to the Laundry Room?"

I am the king of bad taste

Any chances of pursuing a second career as a food critic appear to be dashed.

Not that I don't meet most of the requirements. I like to eat. I *really* like to eat when someone else is picking up the tab.

I chew my food carefully and don't talk with my mouth full.

The Kitchen

What else, you ask, is required?

There is evidence to suggest that my incredibly discriminating taste, and taste buds, are not as discriminating as they used to be.

The other night, Neetha asked me to get out the croutons for the Caesar salad she was making.

I found an open box at the back of the cupboard. Best to use up the old stuff first, I reasoned, before opening a new box.

I popped a crouton into my mouth. Crunched it up. Swallowed it.

Something about it didn't taste quite right.

It seemed, oh, I don't know, a bit *too* spicy. Granted, it was a *Caesar salad* crouton. It was supposed to have a bit of a kick.

Maybe it was just that ONE that tasted funny. Or maybe it was me.

So I reached into the box again and pulled out a handful of them like they were Smarties, and popped them into my mouth.

I chewed them up, moved them all around in there. Let their little spices dance upon my tongue.

Boy, these definitely did not taste like the regular croutons. So I checked the box. Same brand we always buy.

Just to be sure, *absolutely* sure, I tried just one more. I was convinced. Something was not right. We'd either bought the wrong kind, or the company had made up a batch with the ingredients all out of sync.

I held one of them up to Neetha, who was busy tearing up the romaine.

"Try this," I said, tossing one into her mouth.

She took one chew and this horrible expression came over her face. Her mouth and eyes and nose all changed positions.

"Bleccchhh!" she said. "Ohhh!"

"Don't you think it tastes a bit funny?" I said.

"Bleccchhh!" she said again. "They've gone RANCID!"

It took a moment for this to sink in. "Rancid?" I said.

"Didn't you try one?" she asked.

"Well," I said, "as a matter of fact, I, uh, did try one."

She looked in the box and noticed quite a few of them were gone. "Just one?" she asked.

"Perhaps it was more than one."

"Couldn't you tell before you'd eaten half the box?"

"Well, *of course* I could tell," I said. "That's why I asked you to try one. I noticed immediately that something was a bit off."

The priority here had seemed to be putting up a good defence, to prove that while I had eaten a rancid crouton, I did not have the IQ of one. But then I began to realize there were other considerations.

I could see the headline: *Ate box of rancid croutons, stupid man meets end.* With one of those little drop-headlines after it: *Never realized dream to be food critic.*

Was this any way to check out? Done in by a few cubes of dried bread? Where was the dignity in this?

I poured a large glass of milk, figuring it was good and wholesome, and whatever deadly things were at work in my stomach, the milk would take care of it.

I drank some down, then stuck my nose into the glass. I handed it to Neetha.

"Does this smell okay to you?"

Our food items need expiry beepers

Food industry, please take note.

Expiry dates on perishable foods don't go far enough. In our house, we want to know more than the dates at which our bacon, sour cream, salad dressings, and milk are "best before." We want to know when we can throw these items into the garbage without feeling guilty.

We were grocery shopping the other day when I went to toss some bacon into the cart.

"We have bacon," Neetha said.

"I know," I said, "but it's no good."

Let's see if we can analyze these comments, particularly those made by the person identified as "I."

What "I" is saying is: "I have seen bacon in the fridge, determined

that it is past its prime, that it is unfit for human consumption, judging by the fact that it is the color of broccoli, and have closed the fridge door, leaving said bacon inside, acknowledging that I lack the will to remove it from said appliance and dispose of it."

After all, no one likes to waste food, even food that's ready for the waste container. But you can only hang on so long to stuff you know will never be eaten. In fact, there are certain risks in hanging on to it.

"Hey, is anybody going to eat this leftover spinach soup?"

"DON'T EAT THAT!"

"Okay, okay, don't have a hairy. If you want to eat it, fine."

"EAT it? Are you kidding? NOBODY can eat it. It's left over from the sovereignty referendum victory party."

"That's only five days."

"The FIRST referendum. And by the way, it's cream of cauliflower soup."

Once, and this is the absolute truth, Neetha took some chicken from the back of the freezer. I saw the label was from a store we don't shop at anymore.

"That chicken," I said, "is from our last house."

"Pardon?"

"Those breasts moved with us," I said. "That would make them at least eighteen months old."

We were unsure whether frozen chicken is good after a year and a half, but I can tell you that night we had dial-a-dinner. Sometimes you *have* to throw stuff out.

We have a lovely collection of antique salad dressings. Peppercorn Ranch, Caesar, Thousand Island Lite, Italian. All these little bottles are tucked out of the normal range of vision in the bottom shelf on the refrigerator door.

I haul out an oil and vinegar while Neetha shreds lettuce. "This one says February 1991."

"Pitch it," says Neetha, a person of strong character.

I try the Ranch. "July '95."

"Open it and see," Neetha says. For salad dressings, only a couple of years past the expiry date is right off the vine in our house.

"Smells fine."

"You can put it on yours," Neetha says.

A good place for expired food to hide is at the back of the lower shelves in the fridge. This is the Westinghouse equivalent of your car's blind spot. You can't really find out what's back there unless you get down on your knees, or ask the kids to investigate. It's here you'll find leftover slices of pizza that have fossilized or carrots the consistency of bungee cords.

Maybe instead of stamping foods with labels that say "May pitch with clear conscience after (date goes here)," all perishable items should be equipped with beepers that go off, much like a chirping smoke detector with an old battery, when they become as appetizing as an old tube sock.

Hey, it's just a suggestion. And here's another. If you're coming to our place for dinner, bring your own salad dressing.

The Rice Krispie Scam

This had all the promise of one of those magical father-daughter moments.

Paige had just put me through an interrogation about why SHE doesn't find Doritos in her lunch box when her friend Samantha gets them in *her* lunch, because Doritos are *so* good, especially the ones with cheese on them, when she pulled one of the kitchen chairs over to the cupboard.

She stood on it and reached in for a mega-size box of cereal and a sorely neglected bag of marshmallows that, if dropped to the floor, would break your toe.

"Let's make some Rice Krispie squares," she said. "You could put some of *them* in my lunch."

"I don't think I know how to do that," I said. I can open a can of soup, I can boil water for pasta, but the making of Rice Krispie squares struck me as a trip into uncharted territory.

One day my wife Neetha and a friend were chuckling over the culinary ineptitude of someone who had called in a panic one afternoon to ask what temperature to set the oven at to bake Rice Krispie squares.

I couldn't figure out why this was so funny, until Neetha explained that, while you do melt the marshmallows separately, you don't put Rice Krispie squares in the oven.

"Oh," I said. "I knew that."

So now, I could at least call on that experience. *The oven is a no-no.* But there was still so much else I didn't know.

"Why don't you make them when your mom gets home?" I suggested.

"*Daaaaadddddddd,*" Paige said. "The directions are right here on the side of the box."

I took a look. I had to admit, it didn't look all that confusing. So we counted out forty marshmallows into a large bowl, threw in a huge glop of butter, then put the bowl into the microwave on low heat to soften it all up.

We checked it a couple of times and found, to my astonishment, that this actually worked. Once the marshmallows were really gooey, we took out the bowl and prepared to add the cereal.

We dodged a bullet here, to be sure. Paige checked the box and read that six cups of cereal were required, but I pointed out to her that we were using the extra-large measuring cup, which was really two cups. So she poured *three* of these, loaded with Rice Krispies, into the soft marshmallows and butter, added a bit of vanilla, and together we attempted to mix it up.

This proved something of a challenge. At one point, we had, hanging in mid-air from a wooden spoon, a basketball-sized glump of marsh-mallowy cereal. One good swing and we could have sent this sucker flying across the room. It looked like something Mel Gibson would club an enemy with in *Braveheart*.

Fingers were required to pry this mess from the spoon and back into the bowl for further mixing. Finally, we manoeuvred the concoction into a glass tray, where we flattened it out, sucking leftover Rice Krispies and stringy, elastic bits of marshmallow off our thumbs.

"You won't forget," she said, "to put some of these in my lunch tomorrow? It's really important."

"Of course not."

And I thought, Boy, this is wonderful. This is the stuff childhood memories are made of. I could picture Paige at school, opening her lunch box and seeing two Rice Krispie squares there. She unwraps the cellophane around them, holds them between her sticky fingers, and takes that first, delectable chewy bite.

Years from now, she'll remember the taste of those squares and the time she spent with her father making them. And warm, sentimental feelings will —

"This is great," Paige said as we cleaned the bowl. "Now, when I get to school, I can trade the Rice Krispie squares for Samantha's Doritos. Thanks, Dad, you're the best."

Juan Valdez and a nice cuppa tea

Coffee intimidates me.

It hasn't always been this way. Used to be, I was only intimidated by wine lists ("Does it have a duck on the label?"), imported ales ("Boy, it sure is dark!"), foreign foods ("Vermicelli? You want me to eat VERMICELLI? Don't you have any PASTA?"), and fancy desserts ("No mousse for me, I'm a vegetarian").

But coffee was simple. If you were dining out, and you wanted a coffee, you'd ask your waiter: "Could I have a coffee?"

No need for a B.A. in beans back then. And your waiter knew just what you were talking about. He'd scurry off (or, in the more expensive restaurants, stroll) and return with a heavy white mug filled with exactly what you'd asked for: Coffee.

Those days are over.

Coffee is no longer a drink, but an art form. It has its own language. Do you want an espresso? A latté? A café au lait? A mocha? A cappuccino? A DECAF cappuccino? Where are the beans from? What altitude were they grown at? Is the froth too airy? Is the espresso long or short? Did we mention filters?

The other day I had a café au lait, and then the next day ordered a latté. I did not know what a latté was, but I wasn't about to ask, because then it would become obvious I was a caffeine ignoramus. Anyway, I drank the latté, and began to think they'd actually slipped me an au lait, but then again, for all I know, it might just have been a coffee with a lot of milk in it.

Sometimes, with someone I know really well, I'll reveal my ignorance in a quest for education. My friend David knows everything about coffee, about beans, about how you grind the beans, about where you put them after you grind them, and all about how you should *talk* to your beans, like we used to do with plants, to get them in the right frame of mind before you toss them in the grinder. So when I have a question about coffee, I phone him, like I did the other day:

"I've got half a pot of coffee that's been sitting here on the stove since last night, or possibly the night before, and wondered, if I pour myself a cup, how long should I nuke it for?"

My friend Bob isn't much better. When he comes over for a coffee, and I offer to dust off the cappuccino-maker Neetha won a few years ago in some radio station contest, and make something really impressive, he says: "Have you got any Maxwell House?"

He's the same in public. Neetha and I and Bob and his wife Pat went to one of those designer coffee bars that are everywhere these days. The waitress went around the table taking orders, and words like "latté" and "au lait" (I thought perhaps one of us had been mistaken for a bullfighter) and "Colombian" were being tossed about, until she got to Bob, who set his menu aside and said: "Just give me a cup of whatever's closest to A&P instant."

I wondered what Juan Valdez would make of all this, so I put in a call.

"You'd think," he said, "with the millions that people are making off coffee these days, they could give me something better to get around on than this stinking donkey. Just because I'm this simple, charming bean farmer doesn't mean I wouldn't mind riding around in an air-conditioned Lexus, for cryin' out loud."

I asked if he'd sampled any of the new specialty coffees.

"Let me tell you something," he said. "You spend your life picking beans, looking at beans, taking beans to market, you come home at the end of the day, all you want is a nice cuppa tea."

The Friday night what-to-eat fight

It is six o'clock, and it is a Friday, and neither Neetha nor I has remembered to take anything out of the freezer, and suggestions of things that *could* be made that don't have to be thawed (e.g., breakfast cereal) have made the kids drop to the floor, clutching their sides and writhing in pain, and since no one really has the energy at the end of the week to hoist a box of corn flakes anyway, it looks like we're going out.

The Kitchen

Dining out with four people with totally different tastes is bad enough, but going out at 6 p.m. on a Friday, when every other family on the planet also seems bent on finding a table for four (at least), is madness.

Spencer and Paige vote to go to their favourite burger place. "I can't face a burger," Neetha says. I agree. We are adamant. No burgers. We would rather share quarters with a cow than have to eat one. Neetha says: "Let's go East Indian."

"Okay!" says Spencer, who's never met a spice he didn't like.

"Uh, gee," says Paige, panic in her voice, "isn't there anything else?"

So I suggest chicken, the perfect compromise. I could really go for a quarter-chicken.

"I had chicken for lunch," Neetha says.

"I hate that place," says Spencer.

So I wheel into a roadhouse-type eatery that has a varied menu. There is a lineup. Neetha checks and reports it will be at least forty-five minutes to get in. The kids are already starting to dine on the car upholstery, so we pass.

The next joint is the same. No non-smoking tables at all, but in thirty minutes they can seat us in the middle of the Smokers' Rights Association's annual meeting.

Back in the car. Neetha and I think we might be able to get into the fish and chip place. "It's a genuine English fish and chip place," we say, by way of encouragement. We figure if we don't mention the mushy peas (even I don't want to think about the mushy peas), maybe they'll go for it.

From the back seat: "GACK! BLECCHH!" Most of the protesting is from Spencer, who claims to *hate* fish.

"Don't worry," we tell him. "It's not like that's ALL they have. There's other stuff on the menu."

So, reluctantly, he agrees to give it a try. We give our name to the hostess. Only a ten-minute wait this time. And what do you know, we are right, they DO have more than just fish and chips.

They have haggis.

One could get tough and tell a child, Hey, this is dinner, you should be *thrilled* to be going out, you're eating it. But haggis? Did we really want the child welfare authorities involved?

Back in the car. Three guesses where we end up. Spencer and Paige have no trouble deciding what to order at the burger place, but Neetha and I keep staring at the menu, as though the words "fettucine primavera" will magically appear where now we can read only: "Happy Meal."

"I can't eat ANY of this," I say.

"Neither can I," Neetha says. "So what are we doing here? Why have we caved in once again?"

Suddenly, I have a plan. "You stay here and order the kids something, I'll go back and get take-out fish and chips and bring it here."

And I am gone, and back, with the fish, smuggling it into the burger place like it's a neutron bomb, before the kids are even halfway through their dinner.

Spencer looks at my big piece of fish and asks, "Could I just try a tiny bit of that?"

I break off a chunk and give it to him. His eyes light up. He beams. "Boy, this is DELICIOUS!"

If you think this will somehow make the next Friday night easier, you are mistaken.

Spousal Relations and Misinterpretations

The Bedroom

Marital tip:
Don't play Nintendo in bed

There was plenty of reason to think that it wouldn't work.

I mean, there we were, getting married back in 1977, and portents of doom were everywhere. Not the fact that Neetha and I were fresh out of school and had no jobs. No big deal there.

But Elvis Presley had just died. And then, on the eve of our nuptials, Groucho Marx bought the farm.

If that doesn't signal trouble ahead, I don't know what does. The death of the king of rock and roll, and the passing of arguably the funniest man to have ever lived, just before you're about to take the plunge, can hardly be taken as a good omen.

But somehow we've made it across the years. For part of one recent month, we were apart. Neetha and the kids had an extended cottage holiday while I came back home. The first day back we talked on the phone three times. She was up there when an alleged meteor shower occurred, and kept Spencer and Paige up way past their bedtimes so they could see it. I knew the phone would ring sometime after 11 p.m. with a report.

"It was a bust," she said. I was watching *Mr. Bean* and, as she recounted her story of how the kids stretched out on the grass for an hour to see a measly three shooting stars, I told her how Mr. Bean was trying to get past a little old lady moving at a snail's pace down a flight of stairs. And that I'd cut the lawn, and had to buy a new weed trimmer.

This is the kind of important conversation that fills more time than you can ever imagine, until you look at your long distance bill at the end of the month. But we have spent so much time being a team that when I'm home alone I seem to wander around trying to figure out what I should be doing. I can't get to sleep. I stay up and watch an original episode of *The Outer Limits*, the one where an alien made of pure electricity wreaks havoc with a radio station, which, let me tell you, seemed a lot scarier when I watched it as a kid.

As much as ever, I need to talk to her. Her tireless good nature always bails me out.

It can manifest itself any time. We were driving along the gravel road that leads to the cottage and Neetha waved to some people walking along the shoulder.

"Who's that?" I asked.

"I don't know," Neetha said.

"Then why are you waving at them?"

"I wave to everyone up here. It's called *being neighbourly*," she said pointedly.

"Well, stop it."

"Oh shut up."

As you can tell from this exchange, I know a lot about how to make a marriage work. That's why, after twenty years, I'm qualified to offer the following basic rules for a successful life together:

- Never stir something that she has going on the stove.
- Never, ever, hook up the Nintendo in the bedroom.
- When you're telling your spouse about a friend who was complaining to you about all the terrible things *his* wife does, be ready with something good when she asks: "And what did you say about *me?*"
- Give her time to put on her seatbelt when you're backing out of the driveway after you've been sitting out front of the house for three minutes waiting to go.
- Ask her every once in a while if she's bought new eye shadow. Just once you might be right, and you'll look like a prince. Not that this will make up for all the other times, when you looked like a turnip.

- Always ask how her workday was, without flipping through the channels while she answers.

I hope your luck is better than mine at sticking to these rules. I've failed miserably at them, but we're still together, so it's clear I either have some redeeming features hidden somewhere, or Neetha's just got low standards. If you ask her, she'll say the latter.

Elvis and Groucho may be gone, but we're still rockin' and trying to see life as one big joke. If you happen to see us drive by, she's the one waving.

Dirty weekend means newsprint on our fingers

READER CAUTION: *The following deals with mature subject matter and may not be appropriate for younger readers, particularly newly married couples who have not yet started a family.*

Neetha and I decided to go away for a weekend at the cottage without Spencer and Paige, who were thrilled to be looked after by our beloved friend Doris, who takes them on incredibly exciting adventures like municipal bus rides.

Our friends snickered when we told them of our plans. "Ha, ha," they said. "Nudge nudge, wink wink."

You couldn't help but feel cheap.

But I must confess, I feel an obligation to let the world in on what we did, no matter what embarrassment it may cause us. When it comes to keeping a marriage fresh, and that's just what you could be doing if you follow our example here, you can't hide behind modesty.

So here goes.

(If you're a REALLY young reader, hand this book over NOW to your parents and say: "I'm sorry, but I really don't think I'm old enough for this.")

On Saturday morning, we got up at 10:16.

We did not wake up to the sound of Power Rangers, or to Paige singing her favourite song from the *Show Boat* cast recording, "Can't Help Lovin' Dat Man," or to the beeping and shooting noises of Spencer's Alien-hunting Hovertread vehicle (action figure not included).

We woke to the sound of light rain hitting the roof. And saw the time.

"It's 10:16," I said.

"I don't believe it," Neetha said.

Not since Spencer's birth more than a decade ago had we slept in until 10:16 a.m., unless it was because we'd already been up at 3 a.m. with a sick youngster and not gone back to bed until 7:30.

We lay there a couple of minutes, relishing this moment and debating whether to call Ripley's.

If you aren't already shocked by our conduct, I will tell you the other really outrageous thing we did.

We headed into Owen Sound, bought the Saturday papers, and went to a charming little restaurant where we ordered cheeseburgers and fries.

Neetha and I divvied up the papers. I learned that Dunkin' Donuts has been planting microphones in its restaurants, in case any spies from Tim Horton's come in trying to break the cruller code. I found out Russia's military secrets may be up for sale. I checked the local paper's classifieds and spotted several upcoming farm machinery auctions.

"Need a combine?" I asked Neetha.

All the stories I usually intend to read later but never do I read right then.

Neetha pointed out a story about how kids, if they get a No from one parent, will try to get a Yes from the other. "You have to read this," she said, handing it across the table.

I did.

At one point, I had to leave the restaurant to feed more coins into the meter. We were there quite a while, spreading papers out at our feet, trading sections, sipping coffee.

It was glorious.

I told a married friend of mine, a married friend who does not yet have any children, that Neetha and I had this wonderful time, reading newspapers for more than an hour while we nibbled on fries and pickles and bites of burger.

This friend looked at me like I was a complete idiot. "You went away and THAT'S what you did."

"Oh, no," I said, a twinkle in my eye. "We had naps, too."

It's a good thing we were back home with the kids the next day. We couldn't have handled much more excitement.

Oh sure, we did do some other things, but they're so boring compared to what I've already described that if I told you, you'd stop reading right now.

Fear of fetching

"Have you locked up?" Neetha asked.

She was under the covers. She had pulled them up to her chin, and her head was on the pillow.

"Yes," I said. I was sitting on the edge of the bed, still dressed, but pulling off my socks and unbuttoning my shirt. I had the remote in my hand and was doing my usual troll through the channels, not so much looking for something to watch, but just trying to drive Neetha crazy.

"You locked the side door, too?" she asked.

"Yes," I said.

"What about the lights?" she asked. "Did you turn off the lights?"

Zap. CBC news. Zap. *Baywatch*. Zap. CNN. Zap. The Shopping Channel, where the non-stop sales pitches are actually broken up with *commercials*.

"Yes," I said. "I turned off the lights."

She thought about this for a moment. "Did you turn back the heat?"

Perhaps you would have become suspicious before now. Maybe

when she asked about whether the side door was locked, your alarm would have gone off. But when we got to the turning-back-the-heat question, *that*'s when I knew what she was up to.

She wanted something from downstairs.

But like many spouses, Neetha hates to ask for something directly. She likes to mosey around a bit, sneak in her request. After all, if you come straight out with "Go downstairs please and get me my purse" or "Would you mind getting me a glass of water?" there's the chance you'll get a very direct: "What did your LAST slave die of?"

But when you dance around it, when you can actually persuade your spouse that he has a reason to go downstairs, and, by the way, while you're down there could you do me this small favour? you stand a better chance of success.

So, knowing what her game was, I said: "Yes, I turned back the heat."

She was quiet again for a moment, plotting her strategy. "Are you sure?" she asked.

"I have done," I said, "absolutely *everything* that needs to be done downstairs. The heat is back, the lights are off, the doors are locked, the stove is off, the TV is off. The breakfast dishes are out. Slices of bread, encased in individual protective sleeves to keep them fresh, are already in the toaster. There is nothing, absolutely *nothing* for me to go back downstairs for."

Neetha considered this a moment, then said: "I'm thirsty. Get me a drink." Sometimes you just have to go for broke.

So I went. But not before Neetha offered a reason why she was unable to go herself. "I'm exhausted," she said. "I can't move, my legs are broken."

Once downstairs, I turned on the kitchen light, reached into a cupboard for a glass and let the water run until it was cold. And then I heard a very disturbing sound overhead.

Someone was walking around upstairs. In our bedroom! And it sounded as though that someone was heading into the bathroom.

Ah-HAH! Too tired to get out of bed, huh?

When I returned to the bedroom with Neetha's glass of water she was back under the covers, tucked in like she'd never even moved. I handed her the glass.

"Oh, what's *this*?" she said, feigning sleepiness. "Is this for *me*? Aren't you kind to go downstairs to get me a drink."

"You got out of bed," I said. "I heard your footsteps. You got out of bed and walked right across the room and into the bathroom."

"No I didn't."

"Yes you did."

"It must have been someone else."

Too tired to conduct a full-scale interrogation, I got into bed, pulled up the covers, punched the pillow a couple of times, and closed my eyes. And then I remembered I'd left the kitchen lights on.

I spent some time after this trying to figure out a way to turn the tables on Neetha. (This, by the way, is how you measure how good your marriage is — by the amount of time you put into planning how you're going to pull a fast one on your spouse. You can only get out of a marriage what you put into it.)

A few weeks after the glass-of-water incident, we moved into allergy season. Every evening, before retiring, I took a tablet to ward off the effects of hay fever, in part because Neetha is the kind of person who does not enjoy sleeping next to someone who goes "Sniff!" every seven seconds.

I kept the foil-wrapped allergy pills in the kitchen cupboard, where I couldn't help but spot them in the morning, when I would also take one.

The trouble was, every night I'd forget to take one, at least until after I'd locked the door, turned out the lights, gone upstairs, brushed my teeth, and tumbled into bed.

"Oh nuts," I would say, throw back the covers and head back downstairs.

On this particular night, Neetha was under the covers, watching the news. I was in the bathroom, brushing my teeth, when it hit me that I'd forgotten to take my pill.

Perhaps, I thought, there was a way to persuade Neetha to go downstairs and get it, and a cold glass of water, for me.

I needed a plan. Certainly, emerging from the bathroom and saying "Hey, honey, could you go down and get my allergy pill for me?" was going to be a non-starter.

As we know, *she* would say: "I'm tucked in, I can't move, my legs are broken."

Therein lay my strategy. Suppose *my* legs and not hers were broken? Well, if not broken, at least somehow inoperative?

It was foolproof.

I worked out the plan in my mind. I'd finish with my teeth, then walk out of the bathroom with a slight limp. I'd say nothing, almost as though I was trying not to draw attention to my pain, so as not to worry her. I'd limp my way across the room, hobble a bit as I turned to sit on the bed, then slide under the covers. Just to be sure, I'd wince a bit.

Neetha would say: "What did you do to yourself? Did you hurt your leg?"

And I'd say: "I don't know what it is, just a sprain or something, but BOY does it ever hurt." A sharp intake of breath for dramatic purposes. Then: "Oh drat! I forgot my allergy pill!" I'd make a valiant effort to get out of bed.

Neetha would say: "Just stay there! I'll get it for you."

I'd make a feeble protest, but she'd be out of bed in a flash.

It was perfect.

I did one practice walk across the bathroom to make sure my limp looked authentic. Then, like Olivier preparing to go onstage, I walked into the bedroom.

I limped. Winced. Took a step. Limped again. Never looked at Neetha. Made no attempt to garner any sympathy.

Another step. Another limp. We are talking an Academy Award performance here. I was the picture of a man in pain — Dustin Hoffman in the dentist's chair in *Marathon Man*, James Caan in *Misery*. I could feel Neetha's eyes on me.

She said: "Forgot your pill, huh?"

Looks like I'm going to need a better plan.

Who could forget our first meeting? Well . . .

Every Valentine's Day, I think back to that magical moment when I first met the love of my life.

It was in the mid-seventies, but the memory hasn't grown any dimmer. I was in a bus depot in Peterborough (home of Terminal Lunch), standing by the doors that led out to the bus bay. It was a cold, rainy day, and I was there to pick up my brother, who was coming in from Toronto.

And then she appeared. Stepping in from the main part of the terminal, carrying an over-the-shoulder bag and peeking out at the destination signs on the waiting buses, was this dazzling, gorgeous woman whom I recognized as a fellow Trent University student.

Her name was Neetha.

Suave fellow that I was, I decided to break the ice with an intelligent question.

"Catching a bus?" (If you're looking for smooth opening lines, you've come to the right place.)

"Yes," she nodded, smiling.

I moved on to more controversial topics.

"Boy, it sure is raining, huh?"

This clearly established me in her mind as an expert conversationalist. We chatted about the weather and other things for several minutes. I told her I was waiting for my brother and learned she was heading back home to Toronto.

I became aware that she had killer eyelashes.

And then my brother arrived and Neetha had to run to catch her bus.

Even though we'd only spoken for a moment, there was something about her, a quality that intrigued me, that made me want to seek her out again. It was a moment that stays with me to this very day.

The only thing that could make it any more magical would be if Neetha had any memory of it.

The bus terminal incident has been a subject of debate between us for years. "The first time I met you," she maintains, "was in that English lit lecture."

"No, no," I say, shaking my head. "Yes, we got to KNOW each other at English lit, but the first time we TALKED was at the bus terminal, some time earlier."

"No."

"What you're saying is, you talked with me for several minutes, one to one, at the bus terminal, and have no memory of me whatsoever."

Neetha says nothing. Perhaps it is awkward to admit to your spouse that he failed to make a terrific first impression, "terrific" being defined as something you might recall, even if only through the aid of hypnosis.

I have written the whole thing off to bus fumes. I'm sure that, in my plaid slacks with two-inch cuffs — a vision straight out of *Saturday Night Fever* — I was unforgettable, but when Neetha walked through all those fumes to board her bus, her short-term memory was impaired.

Something Neetha can remember, however, is November 15, 1995, when she placed on our bed a basket of clean, folded laundry.

She alleges that, as I removed some folded towels and uncovered a badly wrinkled shirt of mine, I said something to the effect of: "You've made more ironing work for yourself here, piling these towels on my shirt like that."

To which she apparently replied, after batting those killer eyelashes: "Excuse me? I made more work for *myself*?"

Now, it might seem no great trick for her to remember an incident that's only a couple of years old, but I'm already doing my best to erase it from my memory. The fact that husbands make these types of comments is what led researchers to conclude, in a recent study, that men get dumber as they get older. It is pretty frightening for a guy only in his forties to realize that, as stupid as he is now, he has a long way to go.

Anyway, if you're a man and really want to do something your loved one will never forget, consider learning to iron. In the long run, it'll mean more to her than roses.

Garters make all the difference in bed

"Oh rats," Neetha said. "I've snapped a garter."

This is not a turn of phrase you hear a woman say very often these days. It harks back to an earlier time. It's the type of line you might expect a woman with a name like Velma to say to Philip Marlowe in *Farewell, My Lovely*, to distract him long enough for her to reach into her handbag for her .45 to plug him full of holes.

It's also the kind of comment that you might expect that, when made by a wife, would get a husband's attention. And while I'll admit my reply was something along the lines of "Hubba, hubba," I was not being entirely sincere.

That is because Neetha was talking about sheet garters. And I offer you my apologies about raising your expectations up to this point.

You see, we've been having some trouble lately, with a couple of our sets of sheets, getting the bottom, fitted one to stay on our bed.

What once used to fit over the mattress quite easily, with room to spare, must now be pulled and stretched and yanked and forced. I have had a similar problem with some of my pants, but there has been no evidence to suggest that the mattress, like me, is getting larger. But the sheet clearly was shrinking, and its corners were losing their elasticity.

Changing the sheets was becoming a two-person job. To attempt it alone was hopeless. You could get one corner on, but when you went to the diametrically opposite corner to attempt the same thing, the first one would come flying off.

After a night's sleep, we'd be trapped in a tangle of sheet that had come free. Sleeping in a bed where the sheets are bunching up has the same maddening feel of a sock that keeps slipping down your ankle.

So Neetha hit upon the idea of sheet garters. I had never even heard of sheet garters, and when Neetha bought some, and I saw how huge and seemingly outrageous they were, I wondered if she was stitching together some sort of Madonna costume for Halloween.

But even I, with my limited understanding of foundation and supportive garments, spotted something amiss with these garters, in that there were tabs on both ends.

"They work like this," Neetha demonstrated, getting the sheet over one corner of the bed, then hooking the two ends of the garter to the sheet and running it across the corner, under the mattress. "The sheet is secure." Not only that, it was stretched so tight across the top of the mattress you could bounce coins off it.

Occasionally, when installing the sheet garters, one will snap free, shooting across the room like a bullet, cutting down anything that stands in its path. While I certainly like getting my eight hours a night on sheets that are held firmly in place, I feel slightly unsettled by all this.

I can't shake the feeling that I am sleeping on a catapult; that at any moment these garters will give way simultaneously, propelling the sheet and its occupants skyward.

Perhaps we will be pitched through the window and deposited in the trees. The injuries could be extensive. How would we explain them at the emergency room? Would we be able to get adequate treatment from medical staff who were doubled over in laughter?

How carefully have these garters been tested? Are they approved by the safety council?

Maybe there's another solution. I'll just carefully take an inch off the length and width of the mattress with my handy circular saw, and the old sheets should fit perfectly.

My feet will be sticking out over the end, but it's a small price to pay for peace of mind.

Some deals you just don't brag about

I never realized until last week how vitally important it is to have a twenty-four-hour drugstore in your neighbourhood. I had, the other night, what could only be termed a life-or-death emergency.

Neetha and I had been out celebrating at our local Italian restaurant on the eve of our seventeenth anniversary. We had all the time in the world. Paige was at a sleepover and Spencer was spending the evening at a friend's house.

We talked about our first place, a basement apartment in Peterborough. Neetha recalled how much she loved the view from the bedroom window. If you lay on the bed just the right way, and craned your neck around, you could make out part of a tree beyond our car bumper.

After dinner and picking up Spencer and putting him to bed, Neetha noticed it was past midnight. It was now Saturday and, officially, our anniversary.

"Would you like your card now or in the morning?" she asked.

It was hard to disguise the panic that swept over my face.

Imagine that feeling, when you're on the subway, reach around, and don't feel your wallet in your back pocket.

Never, not in all the years we'd been married, had I forgotten a birthday or anniversary card.

So, thinking that there was only one course of action to guarantee my making it alive to our next anniversary, I got out of bed, pulled on my pants and shirt and sneakers and headed out into the dark night for the twenty-four-hour drugstore.

Sure, they carry cough syrup and bandages and prescriptions, but they also have a pretty huge selection of greeting cards. This is what you might call the preventive medicine section, because if you buy a card you have a better chance of maintaining a pulse.

So I came back with a card, but it was not, frankly, a glorious moment. Which is why, the next morning, still feeling my neck a bit, I grabbed

Spencer while Neetha was out picking up Paige from the sleepover, and said: "Come on. We're going to the florist. We'll be back in five."

There was a sign in the window of the florist's shop. "Special: Roses $9.99 a dozen."

"Whoa," I said to Spencer. "That's one super price for roses."

We went inside and perused the different varieties. The red ones looked beautiful, but so did the pink.

"What the hey," I said. "Let's get a dozen of each."

I left them in the kitchen for Neetha to find when she got back. You know, real casual, so that when she did finally find them and sought me out for the big hug, I could shrug and say: "Oh those, almost forgot, just a little something I picked up for you when I was out."

"But roses," she said. "They're so beautiful."

It was, all in all, an excellent recovery from the night before. Sure, Dad forgot the card, but he remembered *flowers*, and not just any kind of flowers, but *roses*, the Black & Decker of the floral industry.

Neetha arranged them in a vase and placed them in the middle of the dining room table, where she and I and the kids admired them, at least until dinner the following night. They didn't, to be honest, look quite as perky as they had the day before. "Droopy" and "shrivelled" are, perhaps, the words I'm looking for. "Near-death" might be even more accurate.

"I still love them," Neetha said when I attempted to apologize for them. "But I feel badly for you because I know you must have spent a *fortune* on them."

I was working up another good shrug, a gesture that said: "Honey, if you get only a moment's pleasure from them, then it was worth whatever princely sum I had to spend on them."

But before I could, Spencer said: "Oh, you don't have to feel bad, Mom. Dad got them on sale. They were only $9.99 a dozen!"

I'll tell you this. I can't afford to screw up Christmas.

No excuses this Valentine's Day

One year, when things were particularly hairy around here (like, when *aren't* they), Valentine's Day kind of snuck up on me and Neetha.

This *should* be one of the easier dates to remember. It's not like an anniversary, which is different for everyone. For Valentine's Day, the reminders are everywhere. In flower shop windows, on television commercials, on your own calendar, where your spouse has scribbled: "Forget this day and you're toast."

But that particular year, around about February 13, it dawned on us that Valentine's Day was less than twelve hours away.

"Okay," one of us said to the other, "I've got a couple of minutes today. I'll buy a card from me to you, and an extra one that can be from you to me."

You really have to be in love to forgive each other for this kind of tardiness.

Anyway, what I'm working up to here is a story about Axel. Axel didn't forget important dates, even when he had other things on his mind.

Axel was married to Polly, and I knew them because my mother and Polly were friends. They'd met at college. They did everything together, shared their secrets and their hopes and dreams.

This was one of those treasured friendships that endured. After they finished college, Mom married Everett, and Polly married Axel.

And every year, Muriel and Everett would find some way to get together with Polly and Axel, who lived in Maine.

Sometimes Polly and Axel would come to Canada. Sometimes my parents would go to Maine.

Travelling with your parents can be a real pain when it's hours of non-stop driving in the back of a 1961 Ford station wagon, but it didn't seem so bad when you knew you were going to see Polly and Axel.

You always felt welcome at their house. There was lots to eat. When you are seven or eight, you view your parents' friends' home as a four-star hotel if there's plenty of mashed potatoes at the dinner table.

And I remember Axel as a gentle, decent man. He had a voice like a radio announcer. Warm, like it was coming to you through your favourite blanket.

Of course, once I was grown up, and Dad was gone, Mom didn't get to Maine as often. And after Mom died, Polly and Axel and I didn't really keep in touch that often.

But I did learn that Axel hadn't been well. He'd been diagnosed with emphysema. When he went to the cottage, he had to take a small oxygen tank along.

Polly looked after him with the same devotion she'd shown to all her family. He'd have been entitled to complain about his deteriorating health, but he didn't.

And then, on January 27, 1992, Axel died. He was seventy-five.

The ceremony for him at the First Congregational Church was, from all accounts, beautiful. Axel was well loved by the people there.

In her letter, Polly told me what Axel had meant to her:

"Axel was my best friend, confidant, companion, and true lover and I'm just trying to keep in mind that I was his Number One person for 54 years and remembering to be thankful for all my blessings."

She wasn't looking forward to her first Valentine's Day without him.

But on February 14 there was a delivery to the house. It was an orchid, and with it, a card.

It read: "For all your loving care. Love, Axel."

He had placed the order with the florist on January 12, almost two weeks before he died. He'd put it on his credit card.

I don't think I've ever had as much on my mind as Axel must have had in those last few days. But he came through for Polly.

So guys, next Valentine's Day, no excuses.

Adventures in Underwear and
Other Clothes Encounters

The Laundry Room

Our drawers have no get up and go

"Where are my tights?" Paige, getting ready for school, calls out from her room.

From down in the kitchen, Neetha shouts: "They must be in your clean clothes basket downstairs! The laundry's done, so they must be in there."

And so the journey begins.

Paige makes the two storey trek to the basement laundry room, where she finds a plastic basket overflowing with clothes of hers that have been washed, dried, and folded. She roots around, shoving aside folded tops and pants and rolled-up socks until she finds the green tights. They stretch out like a bungee cord as she pulls them out from the bottom of the pile. Then, with this single pair of tights in her hands, she climbs back up two flights and resumes getting ready for school.

Meanwhile, I'm looking in my drawer for — and I am going to get very personal here — some underwear. There is not a single pair that would pass the What-if-you're-hit-by-a-truck? test.

And yet *I know* I have clean underwear because I can remember pulling them out of the dryer and tossing them into the clean clothes basket, which is, of course, down in the basement sitting across from the washer and dryer.

So now it's my turn to make a trip to the basement — clothed, I would like to point out, in a bathrobe and socks, which is the second silliest outfit a man can wear, next to socks *alone* — and begin searching through the basket next to Paige's.

I push aside shirts and socks and sheets, knocking a few things off the top and onto the floor in the process, until down at the bottom I can feel a veritable mother lode of gotchies.

"Yes!" I cry.

So I extricate a pair and head back upstairs clutching, in my hand, a single pair of underpants.

Perhaps you see a pattern emerging.

We're very good in this house about getting the actual laundry done. The pile doesn't get very big before someone — even yours truly, hold the presses — will throw in a load.

And when the washer finishes its cycle, the clothes will get tossed into the dryer, and after that, folded into baskets for each family member.

The thing is, we just can't seem to move beyond this point. We can't get the laundry back upstairs where it belongs.

I do not know why this is, exactly. I have, on occasion, actually lifted a basket of clean laundry, and it is definitely lighter than a refrigerator or a piano. It is not a physically demanding job.

Nor is the laundry room in such an out-of-the-way place that we can't see these baskets every time we pass by. Sometimes we must actually step over them — in a kind of Olympic hurdle event as the pile grows — to get to the furnace room.

The prevailing theory is that keeping the baskets downstairs is our way of avoiding even further unpleasantness, namely having overflowing laundry baskets sitting, indefinitely, just inches from the bedroom dressers.

When they're in the basement, your laziness isn't so obvious. But when your lack of will to shift clothing from basket to drawer, without even having to move your feet, is so blatantly on display, it's hard to hold your head up.

The one who has it easy in all this is Spencer, whose bedroom is in the basement, only a few steps from the laundry room. A walk to the basket isn't that much farther than to his dresser.

This, ultimately, may be the answer. The rest of us are going to move downstairs and bunk in with him.

We'll call it a family thing.

These jockeys really travel

I've been finding some of my son's underwear in my dresser drawer.

This is a mystery, not only because our laundry rarely makes it out of the basket and into our drawers, but also because my bedroom's on the top floor and Spencer's is on the bottom. This underwear has managed to wind up two floors away from home. This is as hard to believe as Lassie finding her way back to Vermont from California, without so much as a Triptik, after jumping into that hot air balloon seconds before takeoff to save Timmy.

There is more. A pair of Spencer's white athletic socks has taken up residence in my sock drawer.

I have my theories. One is that my son's socks and underwear are on a mission of exploration, a Disneyesque quest that could be called *The Incredible Jockey Journey.*

Another, slightly more reasonable explanation is that Spencer is tucking clean underwear and said socks in convenient locations around the house just in case we say to him, without warning: "Put on some fresh clothes, we're going to see friends."

Then he'll be able to get changed on the spot, thereby saving us valuable time. Maybe I should consider this for myself. Throw a few briefs in the pantry.

But I have had to settle on my third theory (having ruled out, reluctantly, alien intervention), that stuff is being sorted into the wrong laundry basket because, as our kids get older, it's getting harder to tell at a glance which clothes belong to the kids and which clothes belong to us.

Some of these errors have been committed by yours truly, but I'm developing my own set of strategies. For example, when hunting for something of mine, I am forever pulling pantyhose or tights out of the dryer or off the line. I'm never sure whether they belong to Neetha or Paige, because tights, regardless of whether they're for children or grownups, shrink down to exactly the same size when not on active duty.

Now, lesser men would just throw these things back where they found them and walk away, but I am the epitome of the '90s kind of guy. I am unafraid to sort.

So I perform an elasticity test, using the tights like one of those body-building gadgets with springs and a couple of handles. (I had a set of these as a kid to develop a strong upper body. Unfortunately, I did not keep my receipt.) If I can't open my arms all the way, they're Paige's. If I get my arms out straight to my side, they're Neetha's.

Now that Spencer is growing, and has long since graduated from the Spider-Man/Batman line of underwear, his briefs look pretty much the same as mine, but about a third smaller. So in a hurry, mistakes are made and his stuff winds up in my drawer, just as my stuff makes it into his basket, but *never* into his dresser.

He has an eagle eye in these matters. When putting away his clean laundry, he can spot a pair of my shorts a mile away. He will not touch them. He will look for a long stick or a pair of tongs to remove them, or put in a call to the bomb squad and have one of those robots sent in to deal with it.

My big fear is I won't discover a mistake before it's too late. Pulling on a pair of your son's briefs and discovering they won't go above your knees can throw off one's balance first thing in the morning, and ending up on the floor on one's side is not a way to engender much respect from a spouse who manages to get ready for work every day without falling over.

And speaking of Neetha, I mentioned this business of misplaced undergarments to her and she said, with what I would call a suspicious tone: "I was throwing some underwear into your drawer the other day and found some of mine."

So now I'm on to another theory and am calling Johnnie Cochran. Someone's out to frame me. This underwear's been planted.

A Tale of Two Socks

Gather round, kiddoes! It's Storytime Corner! Today's fable is *A Tale of Two Socks*.

The Laundry Room

Once upon a time, there was a pair of green socks. Even though they were old socks, and one of them had a quarter-sized hole in the heel, they were much loved by their master.

The socks did an exemplary job of keeping the master's feet warm and he was very loyal to them. The master felt the hole in the heel was not a big deal. A hole in the toe could be quite annoying, but a hole in the heel, well, he could live with that.

But one day, the wife of the master of the socks (please note here he was master of the *socks*; he was not stupid enough to think he was master of anything or anyone else) spotted the socks on the floor.

"Hmphhh!" she said, inspecting them. She did not see holey socks as something worth saving. She knew that someday her husband would wear these socks when guests were over, take off his shoes and put his feet up, and reveal his naked heel for all the world to see.

And because this was the kind of house where, if you asked someone to darn a sock for you, the reply was "And what colour is the sky in YOUR world?" the socks were immediately thrown into the bedroom trash basket.

"Oh no!" the socks screamed. "We (sigh) are doomed."

Later, the socks' master came into the room. "Master, Master!" they cried. "Oh save us! Oh woe is us!"

Well, the master heard something. Certainly the word "woe" would have caught his attention, because "woe," like "methinks," is not a word you hear much anymore, particularly in the suburbs. He came over to the trash basket and rescued the socks. He knew instantly what had happened and knew further that he would have to act boldly if he were to save the socks, so he went downstairs and hid them among some other dirty laundry.

"Oh bless you, Master!" the socks squealed. "It's a bit smelly in here, to be sure, but we're grateful! We owe you one!"

But alas! The wife of the master of the socks decided to throw in a load of washing and in emptying out the basket she spotted the socks with the hole in them. "Ah ha!" she said to herself and threw the pair out *again* in a trash basket hidden behind a set of folding closet doors.

Briefly, they turned on each other. The sock with no hole said: "Just because YOU'VE got a hole, I get dragged into this mess! It's guilt by association!"

But they knew that if they were to survive this, they had to stick together. They heard the approach of the master, who had become alarmed when he heard the washer start up.

"Master! She tried to kill us again! Oh, do save us!" So he slid open the door, grabbed the green socks and threw them in with the rest of the wash.

And then, because the master was a liberated, '90s kind of guy who wouldn't attract attention by telling his wife he'd thrown the clothes into the dryer when the washer stopped, he hung around until the end of the spin cycle.

While his wife went about the house tending to other matters, like putting away his car keys so they didn't clutter up the front hall table, thereby ensuring he'd blow a gasket the next day when it was time to go to work and his keys weren't where he'd left them, the master folded the laundry, tucked the two socks into a roll and hid them under his shirt until he had them back upstairs and safely hidden in his sock drawer.

"Oh bless you, Master," the socks said. "One day you shall have your reward."

And the next time he put on these treasured socks, they broke through in the toe, so he pitched them.

The moral is: Should you ever feel tempted to tell your spouse where you've stashed your worn-out old clothes, just put a sock in it.

My new, bulletproof underwear

As part of my continuing mandate to keep you up-to-date on important issues of the day through the use of excruciatingly off-putting details, I'd like to tell you about my new undergarment.

You see, a few months ago, Spencer and I enrolled in karate lessons after he decided it would be a fun thing to try, and Neetha thought it would be good if I found a hobby that would burn off more calories than opening a bag of Doritos.

Spencer and I spent several months learning the basics; the character-building philosophy behind martial arts, kicks and punches and self-defence tricks. But only recently have we started trying any of these moves on each other.

And now that we've graduated to actual sparring, we must wear safety equipment. No one is supposed to get hurt in sparring; the emphasis is on control. But because accidents do happen, we must wear a mouthguard, a padded helmet, padded gloves, and foot pads.

And, ahem, a jock.

Now, forty may seem like an odd age to start getting accustomed to wearing highly protective gear over certain parts of one's anatomy, but I never was a very sports-inclined youngster (I was more interested in becoming Joe Hardy than Joe Namath). And anyway, a jock isn't exactly standard issue for male columnists (except in Sports).

Our instructor, Blake, stresses that this is an essential piece of equipment. I figure I'd be safe without it if I could count on being paired with someone of equal ability; in other words, someone else with leg muscles that snap like old rubber bands when raised higher than a snoozing dachshund.

But you can't count on this. Chances are I'll be paired with some-one who not only *can* kick me, but *wants* to kick me. In other words, my son.

So I've had to familiarize myself with this apparatus, which consists of a titanium steel cup that's the shape of South America and roughly the same size (not trying to brag here), and an array of elastic straps that look like something you'd use to secure a couch onto the roof of your car on the way home from IKEA.

Now, while all this cumbersome equipment might look as though it's going to be uncomfortable, I find, once it's on, that it's no more noticeable than as if you had a Metro Toronto phone book in your shorts.

Rather than change at the club, Spencer and I often get into our karate duds at home, which means I get to drive an automobile in full karate regalia. I have no qualms about taking Neetha's car, an older model without air bags, because I feel I've equipped myself with safety features better than anything Detroit or Japan have to offer.

Anyway, I was getting pretty used to the idea of having to wear bulletproof underwear until the networks started running endless TV commercials about "male itch," something that has clearly reached national epidemic proportions. These air at the most appropriate times, like when I have the news on while setting out the kids' breakfast.

Now, "male itch" is not something I've ever been that troubled about ("Oh!" you're saying. "Thanks for SHARING!") but now I'm in an absolute panic about it. What if I'm suddenly stricken with "male itch" while in karate gear and am unable to respond? It'll be worse than an itchy ankle trapped in a leg cast.

Even worse is the abuse and ridicule we men must endure from the women in the family. When my son and I first got our safety gear, Neetha and Paige suggested they could serve as oxygen masks, should our aerobic warm-up leave us too winded.

And Paige says that in French class they're actually learning a song about her sibling's protective apparel: "*Frère Jacques.*"

We come into some money

I've come into a bit of money.

As you can imagine, when a small fortune comes your way, you immediately ponder how to squander it. Should I go wild and spend it all at once? Put it down against the mortgage? Invest it, perhaps?

This all came about in the most unlikely way. Neetha had decided it was time to attack our bedroom closet, to thin things out, to sort out the mess on the top shelf, to pitch clothes no one's worn in years.

Basically, she wanted to get rid of lots of my stuff to make room for more of hers.

The Laundry Room

(Before we were married, Neetha explained that she'd be very accommodating when it came to sharing quarters. "You will get," she promised, "a drawer and six hangers.")

She had hauled out of the closet four pairs of jeans, all mine, and was submitting them to a rigorous examination. These jeans were all in a condition that could be best described as well-ventilated.

"You *cannot* go around wearing these," she said to me, holding up one pair that, if worn, would allow passersby such a generous view of parts of my anatomy (see "bulletproof underwear," above) that it would no doubt violate community standards. Neetha is the kind of person who thinks this can create a bad impression, unless you are a member of a band with a name like Wild Mutant Maggots, which I am not.

"But they're real comfortable," I protested.

"They're garbage."

"They're sort of handy for doing things around the house," I offered as a last resort.

Well, that was undoubtedly the dumbest thing I could have said, given that I never actually do things around the house. It was difficult to justify needing four ragged pairs of jeans in which to accomplish all this inactivity.

We reached a compromise on one pair, however, that wasn't too indecent and would serve nicely when cutting the grass.

(At the Barclays', cutting grass does not count as *doing* something around the house. Unsticking Paige's bedroom window, which we've been unable to open since we moved in here, *that* would count as doing something.)

The remaining three pairs were about to be stuffed into a garbage bag, but at the last second I decided to check the pockets.

And that's when I came into my fortune.

Down deep in one of the front pockets I felt some crinkly paper that did not feel like an old gas receipt. I pulled it out.

It was a ten-dollar bill.

"Whoa," I said.

"I think that's mine," Neetha said.

I reached into the pocket again and felt even more crinkly paper.

And came out with a five-dollar bill, and then a two-dollar bill. How long had it been since I'd seen one of those?

I was suddenly seventeen dollars richer. My head was spinning.

It was pretty clear from her expression that Neetha was sorry she hadn't decided to check the pockets herself, because there's nothing quite so delicious as found money. This is akin to finding the passbook to an old bank account you've forgotten, winning the lottery, or having a friend pay back that loan you have no memory of making.

We are talking pure windfall income here. And it couldn't have come at a better time, because my wallet was nearly empty and a trip to the money machine was imminent.

So here I am, wondering what to do with my fortune. I could buy seventeen 6/49s, on the chance of turning this into something even bigger, but it seems unlikely lightning will strike twice.

I could pick up two or three paperbacks for summer reading, or maybe finally get a decent chamois for the car, or —

"I'm off to the market to pick up a few things," Neetha says. "Have you got fifteen dollars or so?"

I dressed myself, honest

I was looking very spiffy the other day.

New tan khaki slacks. Dark brown shirt. Fancy brown belt. Colour co-ordination like you would not believe. If I were to have pulled up the pant leg just a little above my shoes, you would have found socks that matched.

Like I said, very spiffy.

And what I thought was even better, at the time, was that this spiffiness did not go unnoticed. I was walking past one of the women in the office who has a fairly good eye for brilliant, yet subtle, fashion statements.

"You look very nice today," she said.

The Laundry Room

"Well, thank you," I said. I let go the fact that she seemed to have placed some emphasis on the word "today."

"Jazzy slacks, the shirt, the matching belt. That looks really nice. Very sharp."

"Well, thank YOU," I said. I wondered whether to show her the socks.

Sounds good, right? A real boost to the old self-esteem. A major charge for the ego.

Then she dropped the big one.

"Did Neetha pick that out for you?" she asked.

Not even a snicker in her voice. Not a chuckle. Not even a little smile. A putdown was the furthest thing from her mind.

She was *just asking*.

It was an entirely innocent question. She had observed a man who was not dressed like a complete idiot, and who had not arrived in a plaid shirt, striped pants, and a flowered tie, and she had come to the only logical conclusion.

His wife had dressed him.

I was ready to set her straight. To give her a little lecture. To tell her that the days when men were colour-blind are over. That men have plenty of fashion sense these days. That men know a lot more than that the underwear goes on *before* the pants, that if you're wearing a tie, a shirt is a good idea, too, and that if you're going to all the trouble of wearing two socks, they might as well be similar.

I was prepared to tell her men are perfectly capable of pulling together a wardrobe that doesn't look like they got dressed in a power failure before the sun came up. That there are whole magazines like *GQ* out there because men are *interested* in clothes.

I could have told her all kinds of things. But there was just one little problem.

Neetha *did* pick this out for me.

Not that I *couldn't* have pulled this number together. Let's start with the pants. I had a lot of input into the pants.

I can remember being at the store, trying them on, coming out of the change room. Okay, Neetha was *there*. And she did say, Yes, get those and forget the other ones I was trying on when she arrived, which made me look like a geek. I'm sure if I'd looked into the mirror long enough the geek factor of those other pants would have become obvious to me.

And the belt. Well, the belt came with the pants, so you could say I picked it, too.

As for the shirt . . . the shirt . . . I have no idea where the shirt came from.

In fact, the more I look around in my closet, the more things I find that I have no recollection of purchasing. Where did this jacket come from? This tie? And what about this shirt?

"I bought it for you," Neetha reminds me. "Remember the sale at Ron's? I picked it up for you? Along with those other shirts?"

Right, I remember now.

So. What did I do when asked if I'd had assistance with my wardrobe? I provided a really good "*Harumphh!*" and shook my head to show how offended I was.

It's a technique I learned from Neetha after a dinner guest asked if she'd made the dessert herself, or picked it up at the bakery.

As a matter of fact, I *do* remember the bakery. It was just down the street from the place where Neetha picked out my clothes.

Let Us Entertain You

From Deck to Den

Nobody entertains like we do

Saturday nights have changed a bit over the years. Some say they're not what they used to be. We think maybe they're better.

Before kids, Saturday nights meant parties. Going to a late flick. Maybe two in one night, going from one theatre to the next with barely enough time to get another bag of popcorn.

It meant hanging out in some restaurant somewhere, talking until they closed the place. Maybe going dancing. (Okay, so maybe I was never a *dancer*.)

It was as if you had to prove how hard you could party.

Now, when we get together with friends who also have children, whose lives are a constant whir, we have a different agenda for Saturday nights.

We fall asleep.

One Saturday night Neetha and I had two really good friends over. Steve (the very person who drew the cartoons for the book you're holding) and Dian have four children. We all know what it's like to balance careers and kids and shopping, and chauffeuring short people all over the place.

We had dinner. Lots of chatting. No end of things in common to talk about. Then around 9:30, with some coffee made and dessert plates in hand, we settled into the den to watch *A Few Good Men*, which I had picked up at the video store.

I'm not sure how many of us saw the opening credits. I can't say how many saw Tom Cruise's first scene playing baseball. But I do know that by the time Jack Nicholson had made his first, evil

appearance, they were dropping like flies at our house.

Our guests had fallen asleep on the couch. Cuddled up together, and absolutely out cold. Not even one of Tom Cruise's childish, overacted outbursts could wake them.

Perhaps you think we should take some offence at this. That when you put on a nice dinner for people, entertain them, *have them to your home*, the least they can do is keep their eyes open.

Maybe.

But I think their behaviour was mitigated somewhat by the fact that even before they'd nodded off, the hostess was in Dreamland.

Neetha had parked herself in the chair next to the fireplace. I don't even know if she saw that part early on in the movie, where the cassette is taken out of the case and pushed into the VCR.

She did, however, wake up about halfway through the movie, and asked some of the other barely stirring bodies if she could get them something.

She didn't offer Steve and Dian coffee. She didn't offer them another slice of dessert.

She asked if they wanted blankets.

And they said Yes. At least, with their mouths pressed into the cushions, that's what it sounded like.

Once the blankets were spread out and intermission was over, everyone settled in for the second half of the movie with some good, old-fashioned log sawing.

I'd like to be able to tell you that at least I had the strength to keep my eyes open through the entire evening. After all, this movie did cost $3.50 to rent, and it only seemed right that at least one of us see it.

Besides, at some point, someone might wake up and ask: "What's happening? Is this a good movie? Are we enjoying it? Did we like it?"

But my lids gave out at regular intervals. I only saw enough of the movie to realize the others made the right choice to sleep through all of it.

Once Steve and Dian were awake, and had shaken the host and hostess for several minutes so that we could see them to the door, they had this to say:

"Thanks so much for having us. It was such a relaxing evening."

I'd rank it up there as one of the best. Good food, good company, good nap.

Just what entertaining's all about in the '90s.

This problem was a piece of cake

It is a beautiful cake.

Three layers, chocolate icing between them.

Chocolate icing on the top and on the sides.

The kind of cake that when you bite into it, and the icing starts moving around and dancing over your tongue, your teeth hurt. The kind of cake that when you combine it in your mouth with a swish of cold, cold milk, you reach a state of bliss that the Beatles had to travel halfway around the world to achieve when they saw that maharishi guy.

This is definitely my kind of cake. But it's a love-hate relationship. We love the cake, but hate ourselves for eating it. For eating so *much* of it.

This is the kind of cake that when you see it on the kitchen counter the morning after, you ask yourself, "Do I really want oat bran today? I mean, aren't there vitamins in cake? Look at fruitcake. That has to be good for you, with fruit in it and all. And this is just the same, except where there is usually fruit, there is half-inch thick icing."

Our friends Bob and Pat have brought this cake to our house. It's dessert for the dinner Neetha and I are having for them and their three grown-up kids and granddaughter, whom our daughter Paige steals away to play with stuffed Dalmatians (toy ones, not real ones).

Spencer disappears with the two towering brothers to the family room where they get involved in Super Nintendo NHL hockey. At one point, someone glances into the room, where this child and two men are slapping a puck across a TV screen, and comments: "Isn't it great how well our kids play together?"

Anyway, finally we eat and get past the meat and salad and all that other useless stuff you have to consume while you wait to get to the main event, and it's cake time.

Not only is this a beautiful cake, it is a *big* cake. After everyone has had a slab suitable for chocking the landing gear of a 747, there is still half a cake left.

This is when the ritual dance begins.

"You must take the rest of this home with you," Neetha tells Pat.

"Oh no, you keep it," she says.

"Oh NO! Your guys will eat this tomorrow," Neetha says. Before long, they are arm-wrestling.

We go through this all the time — the we-can't-possibly-eat-this-you-take-it routine at the end of the evening. We even do this at the homes of people who have prepared things for us that they themselves can't eat, due to a restricted diet. The doctor has *told* them they can't eat it, but still we protest: "No, no, we can't take this. YOU keep it, even though eating it will rupture your digestive system and put a further strain on the provincial health care system."

We want this beautiful cake out of the house because we know if we keep it, we will eat it. Okay. I will eat it. And before long, I'll only be able to get in the house through the garage door.

But Pat is persuasive. We *must* keep the cake, she says. And when she and Bob and their daughter and granddaughter depart — their two sons came in a separate car — the cake is sitting there on the counter, whispering to us as we walk by: "Ha HA! Thought you could get rid of me, eh?"

Moments later, the two brothers announce they're off to a friend's party.

"Your parents forgot to take this cake along with them," we say. "You want it?"

"Yeah! Great!" they say, scooping it up. Talk about twisting their arms.

When we wake up the next morning, I'm so proud of how we handled this, how we managed to get this calorie-laden bomb out of the house, that I go out and get doughnuts. A couple of chocolate glazed, double chocolate, vanilla sprinkle, and a Boston cream.

I feel positively virtuous.

Never can say goodbye

If you're visiting at our house, and have to leave by 8 p.m., you'd better start getting ready to go at 7:30.

It will take you at least half an hour to get out the front door.

Neetha and I haven't hidden the coats. We haven't bolted the front door to keep you from leaving. We haven't tossed your car keys out in the snow.

We just never can say goodbye.

It's at the front door, when people are getting ready to leave, that chatting seems to kick into overdrive. (Also, if you have kids and are trying to make your escape, rounding them up and getting them into their snow pants and boots makes putting kittens in a basket seem easy.)

You've probably already noticed that despite redecorating most of the house and dropping a bundle on that fancy new couch for the living room, you still can't get your guests to move beyond the kitchen. But if the kitchen ranks as the Number One meeting place, then the front door must rank second.

We would also include in this, for when the weather is warmer, the front steps and the driveway. Some of our best conversations have occurred while the window is down, the car is actually running, you're in reverse, and holding your foot on the brake.

The front door is the place where you remember to say all the things you never got around to earlier. The front door is where we remember to ask for the Chicken Divan recipe, which we should have gotten the last time we were at your place, but we spent so much time at *your* front door discussing the Bobbitt trial (Neetha's comment: "You better be nice to me") that we forgot to ask.

The front door is where I remember to give you the latest Lawrence Block mystery that I just finished and told you was so great. And when I leave you standing there while I go look for it, you get into a long talk with Neetha about how Demi Moore ever got to be such a high-priced movie star. (This *is* baffling, and could keep everyone here *very* late.)

The front door is where we make plans for the next time we'll see each other. Someone has to go find a calendar.

It has reached the point with Bob and Pat that when they're getting ready to leave, Bob puts on his coat, then goes and sits down in the living room and starts reading a magazine.

"Come on, Bob, let's go!" Pat calls.

It's true that Pat's right at the door, that she has her coat and gloves on, and that her hand is on the doorknob, ready at a moment's notice to turn it, let in a rush of cold air, and head out to the car.

But it's also true that with her other hand she's gesturing to Neetha about something, and Neetha is gesturing back, and they're talking about whether Neetha should wallpaper the front hall (okay, they are talking about whether Neetha should get her *husband* to wallpaper the front hall), or they're talking about Pat's daughter in New York, or Neetha's job, or the time we all went to see *Unforgiven* and how just before the lights came down they started giggling and laughing about something extremely rude, and the other theatre patrons wondered if maybe this Clint Eastwood movie about a guy who shoots a hundred people to death is actually a comedy.

So Pat's hand on the door means nothing, and Bob knows it, which is why he's picked up a copy of *The New Yorker* and found some 60,000-word article on power lines and figures he might also have time to read the book reviews.

"When you're actually in the car," he says, "I'll join you."

Maybe what we should do is invite people over, have them step just inside the door, but keep their coats on. We could get caught up on everything.

As a chef, I've really run out of gas

The list of things with which I can be trusted grows ever shorter.

The most recent example: Eight of our friends, four from the neighbourhood and four visiting from New York, had gathered at our place for a barbecue out on the deck.

Now, just because your're slapping a few burgers on the grill is no reason to think a barbecue is a simple affair. Neetha had prepared an extensive menu of salads, fancy garnishes, munchies, drinks, and dessert.

Seeing as how I am a husband and a full partner in all the major tasks in our household, I was assigned the job of flipping patties. I think it could be argued that, considering it's called a *barbecue*, and I was the one standing right in front of it, I was still in charge of the centrepiece of this occasion.

It's this way in a lot of households. Men who don't know the difference between Dijon mustard and Miracle Whip think they're Wolfgang Puck once you put a flipper in their hands and stand them in front of roaring flames.

The trouble is, when the grill is considered part of your domain, you're expected to maintain it. This includes making sure there is propane.

Maybe you see where this is going.

Neetha timed everything like a shuttle launch. The munchies had been devoured. The salads that were prepared ahead of time were taken out of the fridge. The drinks were poured. And there were eight guests and Neetha, and our kids Spencer and Paige and, let's be honest, yours truly, who were all ready to *eat*.

"Things are going perfectly," Neetha whispered to me. "Time to throw on the burgers."

I lit the grill and closed the lid a while to let things get really hot in there. I opened it just in time to see the last flame flicker away.

"Uh oh," I said.

I gave the tank a little shake. I could have used it to do a hundred arm curls, easy.

"Does that feel empty to you?" I asked my friend John, one of our guests. He lifted it, nodded, and gave me a wry grin that said: "You're a dead man."

Which is worse? Actually running out of propane as your wife's preparing to serve dinner to twelve, or admitting you've allowed it to happen? How much time, exactly, do you need to answer this question?

I snuck around the side of the house and put the empty tank in the car. "Just going out for more pop!" I shouted into the house and disappeared.

This was the first time since moving to this neighbourhood that I'd needed propane, but someone had told me I could get it at the local megastore that sells more than just tires. I raced over there.

"Nope," said the man at the customer service counter.

He directed me to a gas bar a mile away. Back to the car.

"Uh, nope, don't carry that here," said the gas bar attendant. She pointed to parts east. "I think there's a place thataway."

It occurred to me, as I toured the better part of southern Ontario, that after 5 p.m. on the weekend is not a safe time to be on the road. This is when thousands of panicky husbands, their cars stocked with highly explosive gas tanks, are racing to get back home with propane before the guests drink all the beer.

Finally, I found some (propane, not beer), and booted it home, and learned that John (now my *former* friend) had said to Neetha, when she asked where I was: "You mean he isn't back with the propane yet?"

Rather than say anything to me, Neetha's taken the philosophical approach, viewing this episode as a kind of spousal metaphor.

The next time I say, "Honey, I'm out of gas," I can guarantee her response will be: "And how are we for propane?"

Post-party stress syndrome

There's too little research being done in the area of post-traumatic stress syndrome. Oh sure, you hear about it with regard to soldiers coming back from the Persian Gulf War, that kind of thing, but what about the rest of us? Particularly those of us who've just gone through hosting a child's birthday party?

In the absence of any solid research into the effects of this syndrome on the domestic front, I have turned to beer. I'm not much of a beer fancier, probably having no more than a dozen bottles in a given year. Most of these are consumed after my two kids' birthday parties.

Neetha, who as a teacher works with children every day, can't comprehend my reaction to these events.

She thinks these parties are a breeze. She does not seem to grasp that children's birthday parties are, invariably, attended by large numbers of people who are not yet old enough to hold a valid driver's licence.

I do not know exactly how many little girls were here when Paige had her ninth birthday bash, although if I were to make a guess, I would say it was about the same as the population of Flin Flon. Once your child's guest list gets over five, it doesn't matter whether you have six or 600. The cacophony of giggling and laughing is pretty much the same. The average father's brain undergoes what is known in the medical community as a "frazzle meltdown." There is a complete and total lack of ability to cope.

Last year, we took Paige's friends to a candy shop in the mall, where the kids could go in the back and make their own chocolates.

No one who went to the Persian Gulf saw anything more frightening than a dozen children running around with their hands covered in melted chocolate. Months later, this can cause you to break out in a cold sweat in the middle of the night, screaming: "Incoming nougat!"

So for this birthday we took a few of Paige's friends to see the movie *Toy Story*, where, I was assured by the theatre manager, there would be no huge vats of fudge. But now there was a whole new set of worries, not the least of which was trying to save nearly a row of seats at the hottest movie in the country while waiting for all the guests to show up.

I put Spencer, then eleven, in charge. He was so excited by this responsibility that he immediately asked to go to the washroom.

And there was the potential problem of guests sneaking into the cinema next door to see something else, like *Casino*. Your reputation among other parents can take a real hit if their kids go home and, when asked how they liked *Toy Story*, respond that the computer-animated Sharon Stone hooker character looked 100 percent real.

You also have to keep track of everyone. Let's say you have ten guests, but when you get back to the house from the movie to open presents and have cake, you only have nine. It's not like in high school, where if you got nine out of ten on a quiz, that would be 90 percent, which is pretty darn good, an "A" in fact.

But if you leave even one guest at the show, you get an "F." No one, especially the parent who comes to your house to pick up a child you don't have, will be impressed when you say: "I'd just like to point out that your child was the ONLY one we forgot."

Of course, Neetha had foreseen these types of problems, and came equipped with a small clipboard, checked off names, did head counts every 1.6 seconds, and said later — and this will just floor you — that she'd never seen a better-behaved bunch of girls.

"Didn't that go great?" Neetha observed after it was all over, sitting on the couch, looking as relaxed as if she'd just come back from a week at Club Med. "Not a hitch."

I would have responded, but the beers were already starting to work.

Getting in Touch with Your Inner Barclay

The
Communication
Centre

The fax are these: no one wants to talk to us

We now have more ways than ever to find out that no one wants to get in touch with us.

Our family is on the cutting edge of communications technology. We have the latest phones. We are hooked up to the information highway. We can phone in from anyplace to get our messages at home or at work. We even have a new, heavy-duty mailbox bolted to the front of the house for that quaint old method of getting someone's news, the letter.

If you don't want to get in touch with us, we'll know.

In the past, before e-mail, answering machines, and voice mail, whenever we left the house there was that nagging fear that maybe, just *maybe*, someone was trying to get in touch with us; that while we were out, the phone was ringing itself off the hook, echoing throughout our empty home.

When we returned, we could only hope that if anyone did call with some life-or-death situation, like a dinner invitation, that they'd call back. And, after several hours, when those calls failed to come, we would conclude that someone probably did call, but before they got around to trying us again, they lost our number.

But that's all changed now.

The first thing we did when we moved into this house a while back was sign up for Ma Bell's high-tech answering service. If you've got a message, a little red light on the phone flashes. Or so we've been told. We keep falling over each other coming in the front door after outings (after first reaching into our mailbox and finding nothing but twelve more flyers for discounts on pizza), then race into the kitchen to see whether the red light is flashing. It rarely is.

I have thought about taking the phone back to Bell, to have them check it out, or, failing that, making a few friends at their store in the mall so they'll call once in a while to chat me up. With any luck, I won't be home and they can leave a message.

(To be honest, the light was flashing one day, and there was an honest-to-goodness message, for someone named Rhonda, from someone named Lucille, who said she wasn't going to be able to make the shower, and she was *really* sorry, but hoped her wedding would be just terrific. I didn't erase that one for weeks.)

Once it's confirmed that no one's trying to reach us at home, I will phone in and check for any messages at the office. "Your mailbox," says the voice with which I've become so familiar, "is empty."

A couple of hours later, just to be sure, I try again.

"Your mailbox," says the voice, sounding, if this is possible, just a tiny bit annoyed, "is STILL empty. Maybe you should go find something to do."

Ever since we signed on to the Internet, firing up the computer and checking to see whether we have e-mail from any of our online friends is great fun. There is a wonderful anticipation as the computer boots up, and the excitement continues as we dial in to our local Internet provider. And voilà! No mail!

This is so neat.

So, we seem to be pretty well covered. You can't imagine the peace of mind that comes from knowing, beyond a shadow of a doubt, that no one wants to write you a letter the old-fashioned way, leave you phone messages either at work or at home, or send you mail through the Internet.

And yet, I can't shake the feeling that we've left ourselves vulnerable, that there's some flank left unprotected.

Of course! How could I be so stupid. Tomorrow, we get the fax machine.

WHO NEEDS AN INTERCOM SYSTEM!

Many of the fancy new homes you see going up outside the city, those ones that are finally making some good use of all that farmland that was just being squandered on crops, come with all manner of amenities.

You can get two-car garages, skylights, built-in vacuum systems and foyers large enough for the Burlington Teen Tour Band to hold its practices.

The really jazzy ones come with intercoms. You get speaker units and little buttons that connect all the rooms in the house. If Uncle Norman has overindulged himself on his latest visit and is now in the bathroom paying for it, you can just buzz him to find out how he's doing. God knows you wouldn't want to go in there.

When intercom systems aren't actually installed, the wiring for them is roughed in. Builders understand that moving is so stressful, the first thing you're going to do after setting up your furniture is make it possible to speak to other members of your family without actually having to look at them.

This is all very nice, but few families I know need it. Most of us have settled for the far more reliable, certainly less expensive, system known as Shouting at the Top of Your Lungs.

For example, if I'm standing in the kitchen and ask Paige to call her brother Spencer to the table, it goes like this:

Me: Tell Spencer it's time to wash up for dinner.

Paige: Where is he?

Me: Upstairs, I think.

Paige: (cupping her hands to her mouth and not moving from my side) SPENCER! WASH YOUR HANDS! IT'S TIME FOR DINNER!

She needs to know his location to gauge what volume to use. If he's in the next room, the equivalent of a local call, one hundred decibels should do it. But if he's upstairs, Paige's voice must actually penetrate the ceiling (wood, plaster, carpeting) so she must shout as though he's standing under the engines of a 747 that's warming up for takeoff.

I wish I could tell you it's only the younger members of our family who conduct themselves in this fashion.

If Neetha needs to speak to me about something, she waits until she's on the second floor and I'm in the basement, where the kids have turned on *Saved by the Bell* (a program that makes *Gilligan's Island* look like *Upstairs, Downstairs*) as loud as it will go because I'm running the vacuum.

Someone shouts: "HON!"

At first I think I'm imagining it. Then: "LINWOOD!"

So I go to the bottom of the stairs and shout back: "WHAT? I'm running the vacuum!" In case she thinks the space shuttle is landing in our driveway.

"WHERE'S THE FRONT SECTION OF THE PAPER?"

"TRY IN THE FRIDGE NEXT TO THE KETCHUP!"

If Neetha's in the kitchen, with the dishwasher going, the fan whirring, water running in the sink, and something sizzling on top of the stove, I like to go onto the front step, or across the street, before shouting: "DID YOU SEE WHAT I DID WITH THE HYDRO BILL?"

From the kitchen, a female De Niro: "Are you talking to ME?"

While it may be a bit tough on the vocal cords, high-decibel multi-floor conversations have proved such an effective means for family members to keep in touch, it's a wonder they haven't spread beyond the home.

Can you think of a better way to ensure good communication in the workplace than getting rid of inter-office phones, closed-door meetings, and e-mail, and replacing them with the good old-fashioned shout?

Try this when you go into work tomorrow. When the boss buzzes you on your line, instead of picking it up, stick your head into the hallway and bellow until it hurts in the general direction of his office: "WHADDYA WANT?"

I guarantee you, this will make an impression.

Our six-year-old masters Call Waiting

The phone rings.

I grab it on the second ring. "Hello?"

At the other end, a very tiny voice. A four-foot-tall voice. A little girl's voice.

"May I speak to Paige please?" she asks politely.

"Just a moment," I say. I call to the family room. "Paige! It's for you."

Paige, who at the time of this event is barely six, comes tearing into the kitchen and tells me breathlessly that she'll take this call in the study. She wants some privacy. This must be Carly, she says. Or maybe Jennifer. Maybe Samantha.

She's on the phone for about five minutes when one of us goes into the study to tell her to wrap it up, dinner is ready.

"What on earth could six-year-olds have to talk about?" Neetha asks. "What are they going to do, raid a military installation?"

So we ask her.

"We're having a secret meeting tomorrow," she says. No other questions will be considered.

We're not ready for this. We knew that someday our phone would be monopolized by our children. When the kids got older. When they had boyfriends and girlfriends.

When they were *teenagers*.

But Paige is not a teenager. Paige is six. A six-year-old who has mastered reading, writing, and call waiting.

Spencer still views the phone suspiciously. He holds it to his ear with caution, as though bolts of electricity may shoot out of the receiver and disintegrate him. Spencer, who can hold up his end of the conversation with anyone for as long as it takes, reverts to monosyllables on the phone. I don't think boys arrange anything by phone. That's what recess is for.

But Paige already sees the phone as one of the key tools in her social network.

She is making her own phone book. This we learned as we attempted to solve the riddle of the Disappearing Post-it Notes.

After employing some of our most brilliant investigatory techniques (which consisted mainly of asking the kids: "WHERE THE HECK ARE THE PADS OF STICKY NOTES?") we found them in a book of white paper Paige had stapled together. Inside were the notes, each pencilled with a name and a phone number.

The other day she got a call. We'd answered on the cordless in our bedroom, handed her the phone, and told her not to be too long. And then we forgot about her.

"Where's Paige?" Neetha finally asked, maybe half an hour later.

A search was mounted. There was Paige, on her stomach on her bed, resting on her elbows, her knees bent and legs crossed at the ankles, with a phone glued to her head. Chatting away. She looked like Veronica on the phone to Betty in an Archie comic.

"Paige," Neetha said.

No response.

"Paige," Neetha said, a little more loudly.

Still nothing.

"Paige!"

Neetha's telling me this story later. "And then, get this, without even turning around to *look* at me, she holds up her hand to me, her index finger extended in the air, the universal just-one-more-second signal."

There are plenty of out-going calls, too.

She has just called one of her friends, her makeshift phone book on the desk in front of her. "Do you have Jennifer's phone number?" she asks. There is a pause. "Would you like it?"

She then rhymes off a number. This is her latest excuse to make a phone call. To give out numbers that no one has asked for.

It's clear some boundaries are going to have to be set. I only hope Neetha and I will be able to stick to them once Paige has let us know what they are.

We're afraid to see her Christmas list. *Cel fone for skool bus.*

You think we're kidding.

Never leave home without it

My friend Bob, well aware of the advantages and security a cell phone provides when travelling, bought one.

He got the basic plan, where you pay a low monthly flat rate, then extra for each call. If you have no emergencies, you don't run up much of a bill.

Once Bob was hooked up to one of the networks, he called me at home. From the background noise, I could tell he was on the road somewhere.

"Just got my cell phone hooked up," he said. "Here's the number." I wrote it down. "Call me and see if it works." So I did.

"&%$#@ off!" he answered. "This is costing me money."

His phone runs off the cigarette lighter, so it can be transferred from car to car. Bob is forever asking his wife Pat to take the phone with her when she goes out.

"You never know when you might have a problem," he says.

But every time after Pat leaves, there's the phone, sitting on the desk by the front door. Pat, not exactly enamoured of newfangled gadgets, figures if she's managed this long without a cell phone, she can manage a little longer.

Bob's been desperate to show that where the phone's concerned, you don't leave home without it. The other day he thought he had his proof.

There had been some nasty freezing rain. Bob was driving his Corolla through the countryside and had already encountered police tending to a school bus that had gone into the ditch.

Ha ha! Bob thought. He called the local radio station so they could broadcast a road report for that area and advise parents not to be alarmed by news of a school bus mishap. No kids had been on it, and the driver was fine.

Farther on, Bob spotted a car that had slid off the road and overturned in a field. Its occupants had crawled out and were dusting themselves off.

Ha ha, *again*! Bob carefully stopped the car on the slick road and punched in 911. Here he was, encountering the very kind of situation the cell phone is designed for! You see people in trouble? No problem! Just pick up the phone! Is this technology great, or what?

Bob says if you could have access to the tape recording of his 911 call, it would sound like this: "Hi, I'm on County Road Nine, and there's a car that's flipped over where — AAAHHHHH!"

This signalled the moment when the driver of the car approaching from behind found himself unable to stop due to the freezing rain and slammed right into the back of Bob's Toyota.

Talk about timing! Bob was *already* on to the 911 folks about the first accident and he was now able to fill them in on another one. Here was even further proof that cell phones are invaluable.

I believe Pat, however, views things a bit differently.

Suppose, she says, Bob had never had a phone in the first place. When he saw that overturned car, instead of stopping he would have sped ahead, hunting for a phone booth or restaurant or farmhouse from which he could place a call for help.

But because he had a phone *in the car*, he had parked at the side of an icy road to use it, and ended up getting his bumper remodelled.

For a while after that, whenever I dropped by their place, and if Bob was home and Pat was out, that phone would still be sitting there on the desk by the front door.

But not any more. Bob's gotten rid of it.

"Hello, is Linfoot Sparkly there?"

Voice mail is such a wonderful thing. You can't help but applaud technological advances that allow us to communicate with people without actually having to talk to them.

But my experiences with voice mail are sometimes less than satisfactory. For example, I recently had a call that went like this:

"Hi, my name is Wiffel Shishman and I wonder if you could give me a call. It's urgent." And then he left a phone number on my voice mail.

I played the message again.

"Hi, my name is Sniffle Wishman."

I replayed it again. I closed my eyes and listened, thinking that maybe if I really, *really*, concentrated, I'd be able to tell what the caller's name was.

I wrote down a few possibilities. Niffel Fishbank. Swivel Kissman. Bevelled Walnuts.

He had said it was urgent. I felt an obligation to call back but just who was I supposed to ask for?

Maybe this happens to you. People leave you a message and everything's clear enough, except for those small, insignificant details, like names and phone numbers.

"Hi, this is Carl, give me a call at siff-nerf-four, two-oh-siff-free."

But this time, it was just the name. Is it so hard to say your own name on the phone? Maybe some people have trouble remembering it, so they rush through it in case they get it wrong. Maybe they're embarrassed by it but, rather than have it changed, they spend their whole lives mumbling it.

Okay, not a problem, I decided. Just call back, say your answering machine's acting up a bit, but someone there was calling for you, and give them *your* name.

So I made the call.

"Hello," a voice said. "This is Lissman, Nissman, Piffel, and Grovel. May I help you?"

"Yes," I said. "Someone there was trying to get in touch with me." I gave her my name.

"Do you know if it was Mr. Sissman, Mr. Pliffman, Mr. Ziffel, or Mr. Shovel?"

"Well," I said, clearing my throat and making my voice all gravelly, "I believe it was Mr. Flrrffman."

"Just a moment. I'll connect you."

Then there was some more ringing, and a click, and then a recorded voice. "Hi, this is Spiffy Clifton. I'm not in right now, but if you'd like to leave a message at the sound of the tone, I'll get back to you as soon as possible."

I gave my name and said he'd been trying to get in touch with me and now I was trying to get in touch with him. If he still wanted to reach me, here was my number.

Later in the day, after I'd been out doing important columnist-type things, like checking out some *Star Trek* toys for Spencer that were marked down 50 percent, I had another message.

"Hi," it said. "This is Cliff Sniffly, and I've got a call here from a Linfoot Sparkly, and anyway, I'm just returning your call. Goodbye."

Now just hold on a minute. Was he making *fun* of my name? Was he suggesting I didn't leave a clear enough message? Because I *know* I enunciated clearly. You ask anyone. I'm one fine enunciator.

I wasn't going to let him get away with this. I called right back and got his machine.

"Now listen here, Mr. Pilferly, this is . . ." and I spelled it out for him, "returning your call which was returning my call which was actually to answer YOUR call. So if you've got something to say, you can call me at siff-tree-fer, aym-ny-oh-sem."

So there.

Later that day, another message: "Hi! It's Wiffel Thishman? I called yesterday? Left a message? Said it was urgent? Are you ever going to call me back?"

Chronicles in Porcelain,
at Home and Abroad

The Bathroom

Spencer's flush with money

There is a penny in the toilet.

When you discover a penny in the bottom of the toilet bowl, there are several questions that go through your mind.

If you flush the toilet, will the penny be too heavy to move from its current resting place?

If it *does* move, is the penny large enough to in any way obstruct the plumbing?

If it does obstruct the plumbing, how much is it going to cost to get it cleared?

Could you leave it there as a conversation piece?

If the penny must be removed, whom can you get to reach in there and get it for you?

And, finally, do you really need the money that badly?

(I feel obliged to tell you that this was a toilet bowl of *clean* water, good enough for the refreshment purposes of any household canine. Had it been otherwise, I would have issued at the top of this story a warning of the type they use on the news shows — "We caution viewers that some of the scenes you are about to see may be disturbing" — whenever they do a segment on Ottawa's proposed budget cuts.)

I am always reminded at times like this of an experience we had when Paige was less than two years old and felt that the municipal sewage system could be helped along tremendously if it only had a toothbrush.

As you may know, it's pretty much impossible to get a toothbrush down a sink or shower drain, but your chances with a toilet are better, especially if this is a shorter, child's toothbrush.

Unfortunately, the toothbrush did not reach its destination, lodging instead just out of reach of the plunger's sphere of influence.

It took a team of plumbers to lift the toilet right off the bathroom floor to remove the toothbrush, which was not, by the way, ever used again.

A penny is considerably smaller than a toothbrush, but when you've been burned once you don't like to take any chances.

So I rolled up my sleeve, reached into the bowl, and grasped the penny between my thumb and index finger. I then dropped it gingerly into the otherwise empty waste basket and washed my hands for an hour and a half.

Crisis averted.

Later that day, Spencer called to me, his voice filled with excitement, from upstairs: "Guess what I found in the bathroom?"

Parenthood provides few gifts such as this. Moments where you know something *they* don't know, and informing them is going to be delicious.

"A penny," I said.

"How did you know?" he asked, coming around the corner now where I could see him, penny in hand. He looked pretty pleased with himself. Here was found money, not allowance money, not money for which he was expected to perform a single task. Not that there's a task in the world that either of our kids would perform for a measly piece of copper.

"I'm the one who put it in the waste basket."

"Why did you do that?"

"Because it was in the toilet when I got it out and tossed it."

If he'd been holding pure plutonium he could not have looked more unnerved. "You're kidding, right?"

"No."

He charged past me and into the bathroom, where the penny was thrown back into the trash and he did as fine a job of washing up as any ten-year-old boy has ever done. When he was finished at the sink, he could have shaken hands with the Queen, his paws were so spotless, though it seemed unlikely that if the Queen needed to use the facilities, she would choose our place.

So be warned. If you see money in the trash can, there's probably a good reason it's there. Unless you're an expert at money laundering, give it a pass.

We're privy to a major conspiracy

Let me tell you about The Manhattan Conspiracy. It has nothing to do with the World Trade Centre bombing. It's more insidious than that.

On a trip to New York, our family was targeted by this conspiracy and I feel duty-bound to expose it. There is a plot, hatched at the highest levels, to keep visitors to New York from going to the bathroom.

We have evidence.

Consider what happened to me and Spencer. We had taken a cab down to Broadway and 12th Street to check out Forbidden Planet, one of the world's great comic book stores. After about an hour, we were back on the sidewalk, and Spencer said: "I need to find a bathroom."

Hey, how hard could that be? We headed over to Fifth Avenue and walked north. Up ahead! A McDonald's!

You know how when you go into a fast-food establishment just to use the washroom, you try to fool the people behind the counter by scanning the menu first? To send the message: "Don't worry, we're memorizing your fine selection of artificial food so that we may ponder our choices while attending to some personal matters."

This was our plan. We perused the menu, then went down the narrow hallway to the men's room. There was a sign taped to the door: "Out of order."

Lovely. Back on to the sidewalk, still heading north, we spotted a hot dog joint called Nathan's. There was no sign on the men's room door, but it was locked. A man already waiting there said, "I think there's someone in there."

Ten minutes later, as Spencer's eyes began to bug out, I said: "Do we know for sure there's someone in there?"

The man looked uncertain, so he asked around and found out that we had to have a key. A Nathan's employee, swinging the key from her finger, approached from the front of the store, providing us with the finest performance of cinematic slow-motion walking ever witnessed by a grateful boy with his ankles and knees crossed.

The next day, Paige and Neetha were with us at the Empire State Building. We'd come down from the outdoor observation deck and were having milkshakes in a main floor diner.

"Where are the washrooms?" Neetha asked our waitress. All four of us were keenly interested in the answer to this question. Perhaps it was the white-knuckle elevator ride down, although some members of our party did comment, on the elevator ride up, that they thought they might wet their pants.

"Don't have any washrooms," the waitress said. "There are some in the basement of the building."

No bathrooms? A restaurant with fifty or sixty tables? And no *bathrooms*? Was this, like, the Third World?

So when we finished the shakes we found the escalator to the basement, asked for directions to the washrooms, and guess what was taped to the locked doors?

"Out of order."

I went to an information counter. Where in The Big Apple, I wanted to know, was a washroom that *worked*?

"We have one on the observation deck," they told me. The observation deck? We'd just *come* from the observation deck! Would we really have to go back to the top of the Empire State Building? For *this*? And once we got there, would it be out of order, too? And would Spencer and I feel overcome by the call of nature once we approached that railing some ninety floors above Fifth Avenue?

"Well," said the person at the information counter, "you could try the deli by the diner, on the main floor."

Yes! We beelined it for the deli, a family of four running in mincing, delicate steps. Here was a restaurant with thirty tables, and one bathroom, with *one* toilet, for all its patrons. Male *and* female.

The Bathroom

We fell in line behind five women already waiting to use the facilities. They were each in there so long we began to suspect that they were also getting their driver's licences renewed.

Maybe this conspiracy is part of Mayor Guiliani's water conservation program. But whatever's behind it, we can offer the following advice to Canadians planning a trip to New York.

Go before you leave the country.

Let's put wheezy gerbils out of work

This is an idea that is so obvious, I can't believe nobody else has thought of it yet.

Picture this: You're standing outside a men's washroom, watching the guys as they file out the door. What are they doing? Now think.

Yes, some of them (okay, *most* of them) will be performing that last doublecheck to make sure their zipper is all the way up. Just as some people have to go back into the house three times to convince themselves they've really turned off the stove, some guys will never believe their zipper is all the way up until they've checked it *outside* of the washroom, where it really counts.

But that's not the thing I'm getting at today. And it's not the other thing men do when coming out of the washroom, which is to hang around nonchalantly while they wait for their wives to rejoin them. This is something that comes with practice, being able to loiter outside a set of washroom doors like there's no other place in the world you'd rather be.

But if you said "They're wiping their hands on their pants" you would be correct. In a world where paper towel dispensers have become as rare as a neighbourhood Eaton's store, men have to dry their hands by wiping them on their pants. This is, for the man of the '90s, the drying method of choice.

We have the hot-air hand dryers to thank for this. For those who don't know, hot-air hand dryers consist of a white or aluminum box that hangs on the wall near the sinks. Inside is a small, asthmatic gerbil trained to blow as hard as he can whenever he sees a pair of hands appear through the little vent below.

It comes as no surprise that this gerbil isn't up to the job. So guys end up leaving the washroom feeling as though they've just shaken hands with Diver Dan. Out of desperation, they quickly rub their hands on the sides of their trousers.

(My wife tells me things are no better for women, but I simply cannot believe they wipe their hands on their clothes. I am of the opinion women never go anywhere without carrying a full set of towels in their purses.)

So, here's my idea: Replace all the hot-air dryers in men's rooms across the nation with, you guessed it, pants.

What I envision is a pants dispenser. Just as you'd pull out a paper towel in the old days, with this machine you'd pull out a pair of pants, dry your hands, then throw the pants into a huge laundry basket so they could be used again. (I think it's important that my idea be environmentally responsible.) And then, when the pants had been used several hundred times and were threadbare and nearly disintegrated, you could sell them at a shop on Queen Street West for a hundred bucks.

It wouldn't matter whether these pants were your size. It would really slow things down if, before drying your hands, someone with a tape measure had to approach you and say: "What are you, about a thirty-six waist, forty-inch inseam?"

No, these could be pants of any size, and I think denim would work quite well. It's durable and quite utilitarian, the legwear equivalent of brown paper towels.

Now of course, if you went to someplace really fancy, say a four-star restaurant, there would be an actual attendant in the washroom who'd hand you a pair of pants with which to dry your hands. They might be 100 percent wool or silk, while if you were only in a three-star restaurant, you could expect some sort of polyester blend.

So, all that remains now is to get the idea up and running. I'll need some big-time corporate investors, and I'm hoping to get The Gap or Levi's interested in sending me all their seconds. I mean, is someone with wet hands really going to care about some crooked stitching or one leg being shorter than the other?

The only real problem will be figuring out what to do with all those laid-off gerbils.

Anyway, if you steal my idea, I want a cut.

Bright lights, big city, hairy ears

We went to Chicago for a few days and I saw something I'd never seen before. I saw hair growing out of my ears.

Now, I know what you're thinking. Chicago is a long way to go to see something like that, especially if you're not also planning to take in a Bulls game or see Frank Lloyd Wright's home or check out the art institute or wander the pricey shops on Michigan Avenue hoping you'll run into Oprah. I could have seen hair growing out of my ears by staying home, and saved myself a lot of money and travel time.

Except at home, we don't have, over our bathroom mirror, the kind of illumination you'd be more likely to find in one of those Ebola virus–type laboratories you see on TV, where the walls are white and everyone's wearing space suits and it's so darned bright you can see what your co-workers had for lunch.

But the hotel bathroom did have such a light, with a four-billion-watt bulb screwed into it. If you cracked an egg onto a plate and held it within three feet of this light, you could make breakfast.

It cast such a glow over my face that I saw things I'd never seen before and, frankly, wished I hadn't.

I was standing at the sink preparing to shave when something caught my eye. It caught Paige's at about the same time.

"Whoa, Dad, what are THOSE?" she asked, pointing.

I counted about four or five of them on each ear, on the outer rim of what they call the pinna. (According to *Webster's*, "the largely cartilaginous projecting portion of the external ear." This is what makes writing books like these so exhausting — the extensive research.)

"Whatcha looking at?" Spencer asked his sister. And then Neetha came over. The last time I'd seen the family this captivated was at the John G. Shedd Aquarium, when they pressed their faces against the glass of the underwater tank to catch a glimpse of the Beluga whales, the only difference being, they never pointed at the whales and snickered.

(This ordeal doesn't even count all the new gray hairs I saw under the light of a Jackson, Michigan, motel on our way down. I might have spotted the hairy ears then had I not been so preoccupied with the sign we'd seen before getting off the interstate: "Prison Area: Do Not Pick Up Hitchhikers." This seemed to speak volumes about the community's level of confidence in its correctional institution.)

Why do guys of a certain age begin growing hair out of their ears? What is Nature's intention here?

These hairs are useless as insulation. They're no substitute for ear muffs. If you're going bald, they're not the hairs you'd choose to grow in long and comb over, unless you want to look like an Ewok from a *Star Wars* movie.

They are, however, marvels of engineering. They stick out horizontally. There is no droop to them. If you let them get out of hand, you'd have a hard time getting through doors. If you could affix small lights to their ends, you could stand at the end of runways and guide in small aircraft.

Anyway, shaving was a little more complicated that day than it usually is, but you don't want to tour the streets of the Windy City with anything more blowing in the breeze than is absolutely necessary.

After we got back home, Paige mentioned to me that one of the two bulbs in the upstairs bathroom light fixture had burned out. I took a look, but it seemed plenty bright enough to me.

The Junior Barclays Make the Grade

Home and School

It's *time* to go back to school

Come late August, there are some pretty obvious signs out there that it's almost time for the kids to go back to school.

The Canadian National Exhibition is on. The papers are filled with back-to-school ads. There are a few cars in the parking lot of your kids' school as returning teachers start getting things ready for the first day back.

But there are many other just as telling signs that it's *definitely* time for the kids to don the backpacks and head back to class.

Here are the top twenty-five:

1. If the kids break into "Hakuna Matata" from *The Lion King* or any other summer Disney hit one more time you won't be responsible for your actions.
2. They've spent the last eight hours using a magnifying glass to set fire to a Terminator figure.
3. Your fifty-gallon drum of sunscreen is empty.
4. The water bill for letting the kids run through the sprinkler is $4,928.98.
5. After several outings to the beach, you find enough sand in the backseat to re-groom all the traps at the Canadian Open.
6. After you've clocked sixty-two kilometres on your Nikes walking around Ontario Place and the Ex, collapsed at home, and asked your spouse to run you a hot bath, turn down your bed, and check that your will is in order, your kids, who have their heads in the fridge because no child is satisfied with *just* pizza,

cotton candy, french fries, ice cream, hot dogs, and pop, ask: "What are we going to do *tomorrow*?"

7. As a math refresher, you ask your kids "What is seven times eight?" and they say "Do we have to do spelling?"

8. The time they roll out of bed is the time they used to have lunch.

9. The only reading they're doing is looking at the boxes in the video store to see if they say "PG" or "R."

10. They've seen *all* the Ernest movies.

11. You discover that the kids, who used to be satisfied with a fort made out of a blanket and a couple of chairs, have contracted Greenpark to build them one in the backyard.

12. *They've cleaned their rooms.*

13. They never miss The Weather Channel, especially the foreign temperatures.

14. Every time you start the same paragraph in your big, thick, summer novel, someone comes up to you and says, "She's not sharing her paints with me" or "He said I could borrow his tape and now he's saying I can't and that's not fair" or "How do you spell 'exterminate'?" or "Remember you said we could go to the comics store, well, could we do that now?" or "What's for lunch?" or "If I don't get a drink right NOW I'm going to DIE."

15. They want you to explain the Middle East situation to them.

16. The Super Soaker is plugged with sand.

17. They're offering to do chores around the house.

18. Having helped them organize a lemonade stand, and then an iced tea stand, and then a Freshie stand, you are now asked to help the kids get set up in a dry-cleaning business.

19. You've phoned McDonald's to see what their policy is on hiring ten-year-olds.

20. All the big kids' movies have already been out for weeks, and the only things coming into theatres now are the real turkeys, like anything with Bruce Willis.

21. The signs-of-spring crafts taped to the fridge are starting to

look a tad dated, and need to be replaced with signs-of-fall crafts.

22. They've caught and examined butterflies, slugs, salamanders, frogs, and grasshoppers, sometimes with macabre results, and are now taking a close look at the neighbour's cat.
23. You've made formal application to have your name changed to anything except "Mom" or "Dad."
24. There's no more Extra Strength Tylenol.
25. When you call them down to breakfast, they shout: "Just a minute! *Regis and Kathie Lee* isn't over yet!"

My first-day-of-school jitters

Spencer's dressed, has eaten his breakfast, made his bed, put his lunch into his backpack, and brushed his teeth.

It's not even 7:40 a.m. yet.

Paige isn't far behind. There are a few Cheerios left in her bowl, and she still has to brush her teeth, but other than that she's all set to go.

We will never be ready for school this early again.

They are eager, yes, but it is an eagerness driven by anxiety. They want to *get* to school, they want to *face* it, because they are tired of worrying about this day, tired of imagining what it will be like, tired of wondering whether they'll be able to find the washrooms or make new friends.

On this particular first day, they are going to a new school. Spencer's entering Grade Five, Paige Grade Three. There's always been some apprehension surrounding starting a new grade, but this year is special.

We moved over the summer, and the level of angst over a different school increased as we approached Labour Day.

The kids have been getting a bit worried, too.

Not since they started kindergarten have Neetha and I confronted these kinds of feelings.

What will their teachers be like? Will the Grade Fives already be into a twelve-times table? How much time will they get for lunch? Is there a crossing guard at the corner?

It's back to school for Neetha as well, who has to be off to work before the kids embark on their new adventure.

As she kisses them goodbye I tell her not to worry, I will walk Spencer and Paige to school, meet the teachers, tell them they have two newcomers.

"When are we going?" Spencer calls from the front door.

"Ten minutes!" I shout from upstairs.

No one has had much rest. The kids hadn't been able to settle down the night before. They lay in bed, staring at the ceiling. I went in to check on Spencer.

"I just can't get to sleep," he said.

"Picture yourself at a railway crossing," I said, "and a huge train is going by, and count the boxcars."

"I was imagining I'd won a shopping spree at Toys R Us."

"That'll do."

Paige was almost inconsolable. She'd gone to bed cheerful, but in the darkness were demons. And I dreamt I was at the office when I realized it was time to walk the kids to school, that I'd somehow managed to come to work without remembering to tend to this one little detail.

But with daylight comes a determination to face this new challenge. By the time I hit the kitchen, Spencer's there in a new pair of jeans and a red shirt. No hair bump. Paige has brushed her hair and put in one of her favourite clips at the back.

Finally, it's time to go. There are a few other parents on the street, some with kids the same age as ours, some with children destined for their first day of Grade One. After ten minutes we're at the school-grounds, which are filled with kids getting reacquainted, hanging off the climbers, asking who they've got as teachers. Spencer asks if we shouldn't check in with the office, let them know we're here.

There are signs stuck to the school wall. "Grade 1" and "Grade 2" and on up. The chaos that was the playground turns to order as the kids line up by grade, then are sorted into individual classes. We are looking for Mr. Kumagai, Paige's teacher, and Mr. Brett, who heads Spencer's class.

Suddenly, there they are. Real faces to go with the names. Joking with the kids, reassuring them, getting them arranged in single file, shaking the hands of the *really* nervous ones — the parents.

On their way in, Paige flashes me a confident smile. Spencer, heading the other way, makes a small, hesitant wave.

And then the kids are gone, the doors swing shut, and one parent is left standing in the playground to fend for himself.

Grade Three math is too advanced for me

I can balance a chequebook. Most days, I can figure out the car's mileage with a metric calculator just like that. There is a part of my brain that can still be called upon to do square roots in an emergency. You know, like when someone shouts: "Dear heavens! Is there a mathematician in the house?"

Just don't ask me to do Grade Three math.

Paige wanted some help with her homework. "I'm having trouble," she said, "with the last question."

I had her point to the assignment in her math text. There was a picture of two horizontal rows of four circles. Three circles in the top row and three in the bottom were blue. The remaining two, in the last column, were yellow. Picture this, if you can.

"What exactly is the problem?" I asked.

"I'm not sure I get what they want me to do."

"Well," I said confidently, "let's read the question." It seemed relatively simple. It asked the student to look at the diagram and derive four facts from it.

"Okay," I said. "I think you can do this. Look at this drawing. Tell me about it."

Paige pressed her lips together. "There are eight circles," she said.

"There you go," I said. "That's a fact. Write that down." So Paige wrote in her notebook: "There are eight circles."

About this time, Neetha walked by. We filled her in.

"I think," Neetha said, "that they're looking for *number* facts."

"What?" I said.

"Number facts. You know. There are six blue circles, two yellow. So one number fact would be six plus two equals eight. Or eight take away two is six."

"No no," I said. I did my best not to show how exasperated I was by her interpretation of a question that looked pretty clearly worded to me.

"It says right here," I said, pointing to the textbook. "*Facts.*"

I mean, *excuse me*, but when you've worked in the newspaper business for almost two decades you tend to know what a *fact* is. The Earth is round. That's a *fact*. The sun will rise tomorrow morning. That's a *fact*. And there are eight little circles in this diagram and that is a *fact*.

"Okay, Paige," I said, "what's another fact that you get from looking at this diagram?"

"There are six blue circles."

"That's a fact! Write that down." And she did. Then she told me that there were two yellow circles. "Terrific! You just need one more!"

"They are in two rows of four?"

"You're done! See how easy that was? And to think you thought you didn't know how to do it."

So Paige closed her notebook, tucked it into her backpack so as not to forget it in the morning, and scampered off. I basked in the self-radiating glow wise fathers give off when they have dispensed wisdom and made that difficult path children must follow through life just a little easier to travel.

Neetha had that look, that "we'll-just-wait-and-see" look.

I hate that look.

When Paige came home from school the next day I was the first to ask her if she got her last homework question right.

"No," she said. "It was wrong."

Neetha explained to me later that, what do you know, Paige was expected to find number facts. And that when Paige explained at school that her own father had helped her come up with the answer, her teacher said sympathetically: "Don't worry about it."

I guess you'll have to add this to the list of problems facing the school system these days. Declining funds, increased workload, bigger class sizes, and parents who haven't a clue what they're doing.

And that's a *fact*.

It's in the bag

Welcome to *Spencer's Backpack*, where we keep you up-to-date on that thing my son Spencer throws over his shoulders every morning on his way out the door to school.

I've already been worried for a while that his backpack has been getting too heavy, in large part because he's been carrying around a three-ring binder of trading cards that weighs roughly the same as a Ford Pinto. This causes the school bus to list over to one side when he boards.

When Spencer became worried that his card collection was becoming too valuable to lug to school every day, he filled a smaller binder with less valuable cards that were still suitable for the daily recess examination.

This led me to the mistaken impression that there might now be some room in his backpack.

Last week, he announced he needed to take a large bag of Lego to school for a class project. Once all the kids brought some in, they were going to be able to build a space port, or a rocket ship, or something, so that several teachers could be sent to Venus as part of the provincial cutbacks.

"I need you to drive me to school because there's so much Lego," Spencer said.

"Since you're not carrying that big binder anymore," I said, "just put it in your backpack."

"I don't know if there's room," Spencer said.

So, foolishly, I said, "Let's have a look."

Spencer brought his backpack into the study and began to empty it. I was looking for the usual things you might find in the bag of a serious student: pencils, notebook, maybe a dictionary.

This is what I found:

One baseball glove, two tennis balls, a pair of worn Thinsulate winter gloves, R.L. Stine's *The Hitchhiker*, with a Garfield bookmark tucked in between pages forty and forty-one, a Doug Gilmour portrait rookie card in a rigid plastic card protector, a black mitten —

"Oh," said Spencer, "there's my other black glove I lost."

— an empty box from the Super Nintendo StarFox game, a Scholastic Arrow book club order form with *Goosebumps: The Scarecrow Walks at Midnight* circled for our attention, six large plastic tires, four medium-sized plastic tires, and two small plastic tires.

Two Pilot Fineliner felt tip pens, two pencils, one chewed, a Brad Tiley Binghamton Rangers card from the Pro Hockey Prospects series, a made-in-Taiwan Reebok Blacktop key fob, four Matchbox-sized metal Racing Champion NASCAR-type model cars, one and a half pencil-stabbed erasers.

A Lego car door labelled Police, a New Jersey Devils Kevin Todd rookie card, a Ninja Turtles bookmark, a Random House book called *Building Bridges and Tunnels*, an empty (thank heavens) sandwich bag.

The packaging boards for eight X-Men figures (Cable, Cable Second Edition, Wolverine Third Edition, Omega Red, Mr. Sinister, Deathlok, Gambit), *Fantazone* magazine No. 28 from two years ago, with the cover story "Batman Returns: The Making of a Blockbuster," a software catalogue for computer math games.

A word-search puzzle in French, a test on geometric shapes (with the teacher's comment: "Super!"), the Official Marvel Index to the X-Men, two issues of *Starlog* magazine (one about *Batman*, one about *Alien*), several other assorted bits and pieces of Lego, including a Lego man and his helmet, and a 60 percent straightened-out paper clip.

I am not kidding.

Anyway, once we had all this stuff spread out all over the study floor, there was room in the backpack not only for Lego for the class project, but his *big* binder. We also managed to squeeze in his lunch.

Bristol board and speeches: A '90s homework guide

My theory, which I call "Homework and Karmic Retribution," goes something like this: If you didn't do your homework when you were a kid, you'll get more than you dreamed of when you have children of your own.

This would help explain why Neetha and I have been so busy with homework these last few weeks. It's not that we're actually doing Spencer's or Paige's homework — they would have none of that — but we're constantly on call, like those computer companies that offer twenty-four-hour support by way of an 800 number.

Some nights it's only a bit of help with a question in a textbook. An integer inquiry from Spencer. A French vocabulary drill for Paige.

But some nights are nuts. Recently, for example, Paige, whom I'd already taken to the store for that old standby, bristol board, was completing her Grade Five display project, "The Beagle," while Spencer, now in Grade Seven, was getting a handle on The Speech.

Now, The Speech deserves a spot on any parent's list of Top Ten Homework Nightmares. The last couple of school years, the kids have each come home with the following assignment: "Pick an interesting topic and speak on it for three to five minutes."

The key words here are not "interesting topic" but "three to five minutes." Oddly, this is the part of the assignment that fills the kids, who under normal circumstances seem able to talk nonstop for several days without any specific topic whatsoever, with dread. How on earth will they fill *three minutes*?

The process goes something like this:

"Would you listen to my speech so far? And would you time it with this watch?"

"Okay, go."

"Teachers, fellow students, today I'd like to speak to you about. Okay. How long was that?"

"Four seconds."

This is followed by huge sighs of desperation.
Meanwhile, Paige is sticking information boxes about the beagle to her bristol board, a product that, despite the advent of computers and calculators, remains the most important educational tool.

Anyway, the centrepiece of this project is to be a colour picture of a beagle from a now out-of-date calendar.

"Has anyone seen my calendar?" Paige asks, coming into the study where Spencer is now having me time his speech again because he has inserted a comma. There is a hint of panic in Paige's voice. "It was right in my room, and it's gone."

"Well, I didn't do anything with it," Spencer says, immediately making him, in Paige's mind, the Number One suspect.

"Were you working on your project downstairs?" I ask. She doesn't think so, but she checks. She enlists Neetha's help in the search. They look in the family room. They look under magazines in the study. They look in Spencer's room, just in case.

The house looks like it's been tossed by an RCMP drug squad.

Neetha suggests to Paige, who is way beyond panic now, that they re-examine her room. They look under the bed, between the covers and the wall. Second and third searches are made of Paige's desk drawers, where she thought she'd stored the calendar all along.

And that's when someone notices that it has fallen behind the drawers, into one of those "desk black holes" where things vanish forever.

Three cheers go up from Paige's room. "We've got it!"

In the study, I look up from Spencer's watch and say: "That's one minute, forty-five seconds. Put in some more commas."

Later, getting ready for bed, I mention to Neetha that Spencer's speech is finally long enough, and that Paige's beagle project, with the photo from the calendar pasted into place, looks pretty good.

"I hope I get an 'A,'" Neetha says.

(Dis)order in the House

Chores

Just another trashy, flashy story

I'd just like to explain what I was doing out on the sidewalk the other day, wearing a trenchcoat with no clothes on underneath.

And if you're the lady who went by our house that morning on your daily power walk, I'd like you to know that there's no need to call the authorities.

Several events conspired to place me on the street at that time, making that kind of fashion statement. They include the closing of the schools for the summer, staying in bed to hear that day's weather forecast on the clock radio, and the July 1 holiday.

With school out, Neetha and the kids are home, and the mornings are (most days) a little less harried. There are no lunches to make, no last-minute homework assignments to find and stuff into backpacks, no panicky searches for car keys, no constant harping at Spencer and Paige that if they don't get moving, they'll be late for class.

And best of all, the alarm's not set for 6:30 a.m. Mornings are leisurely when three out of four are off for the summer. And, as my family would tell you, when the fourth is a columnist, it's not like *he*'s got any pressing demands, right?

So Neetha and I are taking our time getting up, and it's nearly eight o'clock, so I lean over and turn on the radio to see what kind of day we can expect.

That's when we hear the truck.

Not a speeding truck, but the droning, dieselly sound of a truck that's starting up, then stopping. Starting up, then stopping. It sounds as though it's only moving a few feet at a time, say the distance from one driveway to the next, just like a . . .

Garbage truck!

How can this be? This is *Wednesday* and the garbage always gets picked up on *Tuesday*. But we didn't put the trash out Tuesday because we'd just come off a long weekend, when the collection is always delayed a day.

I emerge from under the covers in a pair of boxers and start hobbling my way downstairs Walter Brennan–style. I say "hobbling" because I've reached the stage in life where you must walk around a while before all the joints are properly lubricated. I need to have myself outfitted with a block heater that I can plug in before going to bed at night.

As I reach the front door, I can hear the truck's nearly reached our house. This is when it dawns on me that running to the curb in my boxers is going to do nothing for my fine reputation or my neighbours' property values.

There's no time to run back upstairs for a bathrobe or pants. So I throw open the front hall closet. I see *short* spring and summer jackets. These are not going to do the trick.

The truck is almost here.

Shoving aside hangers to get to non-seasonal items that have been relegated to the far ends, I spot my long green trenchcoat, slip it on, and tie the belt at the front. I open the garage door and drag our two cans down the drive, feeling grit and dew beneath my feet. The truck is half a lot away.

I am a vision of loveliness. Hair bumps, bare legs and feet, unshaven, wearing a trenchcoat. I am an ad warning people not to go into the park alone. "If you see this man, call Crimestoppers."

The guy hanging off the back of the truck looks at my cans and says: "Lawn clippings?"

"What?" I say. "No, just regular trash."

"We're just picking up the clippings," he says, and the truck rolls on.

About then the morning power walker goes by, glancing at me. I think she cut a few seconds off her trip that day.

Sweeping recriminations hit home

We lost our broom.

There we were one day, using it to sweep off the deck and the front step, and the next day, there it was, gone.

A broom did not strike us as any easy thing to lose. It is a good five feet long. The business end of the broom is quite wide. The broom is considerably larger than other things, like car keys, earrings, and sunglasses, that are lost or misplaced on pretty much a daily basis around here.

"Did you look in the garage?" Neetha asked.

Well, of *course* I'd looked in the garage, but I decided to look again. There was a chance, given my track record, that I had missed it the first time. So I searched the garage, scanning for long, dowel-like pieces of wood. Found a hockey stick, a couple of mop handles without the mops, and one of those coloured plastic shower rod sleeve thingies that had been discarded in favour of a much trendier colour. No broom.

(By the way, if you're waiting for me to suggest someone rode off on it, I'm sorry, but this is the '90s, not an episode of *Bewitched*.)

"Try downstairs," Neetha suggested. "You know the spot between the old fridge and the wall, where the ironing board is?"

So I checked. There was the folding ironing board, the upright vacuum. No broom.

I looked in all the closets, then all around the house. The furnace room. That little storage room behind the downstairs bathroom. Checked the garage for a third time.

Still no broom.

"I bet I know what happened," Neetha said. "It was probably out front when we had our garage sale and someone stole it."

This seemed almost possible; it would have been about the most valuable thing out on the driveway that Saturday morning. Was there a stolen broom ring working the neighbourhood? Were hot brooms being taken to a chop shop, broken down into individual lengths of straw, and then shipped across the border?

"No," I said, "I'm sure it wasn't out front that morning."

We called in Spencer and Paige. "Whoever finds the broom," we said, "gets a loonie." They tore the house apart as only two children desperate for cash can. They came up empty.

It was only a matter of time before the recriminations began.

"You used it last," I said to Neetha, "when you were sweeping around the patio."

"No," Neetha said, "it was YOU, doing the driveway after you cut the grass."

We began to view each other suspiciously, each convinced of the other's guilt, like in that movie *The Thing*, where no one knows for sure who the alien monster is.

There was only one way of making this broom turn up. We would have to buy another one.

And it wouldn't do any good to leave the new broom in the car and save the receipt. The old broom would refuse to surface until the new one had been broken in to such an extent that it could not be returned.

We used the new broom for a week. We swept the drive. We swept the deck. We swept the front steps, where the squirrels are always burying things in the flower pots and making a terrible mess.

"I'm going to iron some shorts," Neetha said. A few minutes later she came upstairs. "I found it."

The broom had been tucked in next to the old refrigerator in the basement, directly behind the ironing board. If you can picture a folded ironing board, wide end to the floor, you can see what a perfect hiding spot it was.

But this was not the end of it.

"I never put it there," I said.

"Well, it wasn't me," Neetha said.

Life goes on.

Life's never dull living with The Stripper

Spencer and Paige were both invited over to friends' houses for dinner the other night, so Neetha and I stayed home and stripped. It took us all evening.

Now, I know what you must be thinking. We're not as young as we used to be. What we once were able to accomplish with some speed now takes forever. But it wasn't that at all. It's just that the old wallpaper was stuck on so doggone hard, it took hours to peel it off.

The only household job worse than putting up wallpaper

has to be stripping it. In fact, I've long believed applying wallpaper is the leading cause of divorce in this country, even beating out what was long thought to be the Number One reason for marital discord: stranding your spouse at home after leaving for work with both sets of car keys.

I've imagined the following scenario, where a couple in distress makes an appointment with a marriage counsellor.

Counsellor: So, what seems to be the problem? Someone has had an affair? There are money troubles? It is, perhaps, a sexual problem? Interfering in-laws? It does not matter, we can make it right.

Husband: We've been wallpapering.

Wife: We'd just put up the last roll, and then I wasn't so sure I liked the pattern.

Counsellor: I'm sorry, but there's nothing I can do.

Stripping off old wallpaper is also fraught with problems. But the real tension begins during the debate over whether to even attempt the project. The first thing I have to consider is my track record in wall-paper-stripping, which is somewhat chequered, unless you're the kind of home decorator who appreciates the effect you get from ripping out huge strips of drywall that have become permanently fused to the paper.

You have to be sure you know what you're doing, because once that first strip comes off, there's no turning back.

"I wonder how hard this stuff is stuck on," Neetha said, slipping her fingernail under one little corner of paper in the basement room where we watch TV.

"Don't do that," I said.

"I'm just going to peel back the TEENSIEST bit to see if it will come off easily."

"Don't do that," I said.

"I think it's coming off. I'm just going to pull a little more . . ."

"Don't do that," I said.

"Uh oh."

So what we had then was a room that looked absolutely perfect so long as you didn't notice, right in the middle of it, the huge, shredded strip dangling off the wall. We were now, as they say, committed.

Which explains why two adults, given an opportunity to go out for a quiet dinner or spend a romantic evening at home, chose to strip wallpaper. (This reminds me of the time a couple of years ago, when friends offered to take the kids for the afternoon, and we went to the Price Club to buy a carpet cleaner. And they say romance is dead.)

We'd started the job in the afternoon, and by the time Spencer and Paige received their invitations, it was as though we were possessed. I was actually getting into it. Nothing could stop me.

"I think I'm getting hungry," Neetha said.

"Let me just finish this strip."

"You said that five strips ago."

"Just this strip, and this one next to it. Then I'm all the way to the corner."

"Food!"

Anyway, after hours of soaking and scraping and bagging mountains of soggy paper, we were ready to think about the next day's trip to the paint store to look at those little colour chips.

Which brings us to how deciding on a new colour for a room is one of the leading causes of divorce. Have I told you about that?

Oven cleaner is no substitute for fertilizer

I am not very happy with my local garden centre.

You count on these people, with all their expertise, to guide you in the care of your lawn and garden. They are supposed to *be there* for you.

But not once, in all the times I've been to my local provider of shrubs, flowers, herbicides, and wheelbarrows, has anyone bothered to tell me that you should not spray Easy-Off oven cleaner on your grass.

This is as clear a case of negligence as I've ever seen.

Let me give you some background. The other day we fired up the barbecue for the first time this year. We had some friends coming over and we were planning to dine elegantly on totally burned-to-a-crisp sausages and hot dogs.

When I opened the lid of the barbecue I discovered the racks were covered in several inches of a year-old, black, crusty substance.

This material, which I considered saving to patch some holes in my driveway, put me in mind of Jurassic Park–type amber. If scientists could dig into this stuff and extract its DNA, they'd be able to recreate, in the lab, a living, breathing chicken weiner.

Anyway, Neetha suggested that *cleaning* the racks might be in order (sooner or later, I might have thought of this, too) and she went on to suggest that to loosen this grime, I spray the racks with some Easy-Off oven cleaner.

So, grasping them one at a time by the corner, I held the racks out over the lawn at arm's length and sprayed them senseless. You could almost hear the Easy-Off chewing this grunge right off the racks.

As I was spraying, I noticed that some of the excess Easy-Off that did not cling to the racks was floating to the ground in a very fine mist. Committed environmentalist that I am, I thought nothing of it.

Until the next day, when I found two yellow spots the size of those mysterious crop circles right where I'd been cleaning the racks. Evidently, and to my total surprise, the same chemical that can eat right through fossilized food products can also do harm to living vegetation. Who would have thought?

So now I have two huge spots of dead grass. But rather than tell someone I sprayed the yard with Easy-Off, which can make you look, to some people anyway, like you're a few briquets short of a load, I explain that two dogs the size of polar bears hopped over the fence for a pit stop.

So you can understand my anger with the garden centre.

They're usually so good at explaining things. For example, when I buy weed'n'feed, they provide endless instructions:

1. To determine how much fertilizer to apply, calculate the number of Celsius millihectares of your property by measuring its length and width, using a protractor, slide rule, and abacus. Be sure to subtract from this result the area occupied by your home, driveway, decorative but tasteless lawn ornaments, and any large holes created by chunks of frozen glunk jettisoned from jumbo jets.

2. Estimating that each millihectare contains 3,876,076 blades of grass, divide that figure by the number of weed'n'feed granules it takes to fill an empty Diet Pepsi can.

3. Keep in mind that this product should not be applied three days before rain, three days *after* rain, in excessively sunny or cloudy conditions, or if the swallows have not yet returned to Capistrano.

4. WARNING: Though there may be no taste difference, never use this product in place of bacon bits.

I mean, really. How much trouble would it have been to add something about Easy-Off?

Real men use gas lawnmowers

A few years ago, when Robert Bly's book *Iron John* was all the rage, men were going off to wilderness retreats where they painted their faces like Mel Gibson in *Braveheart*, beat drums, sat around campfires, and got in touch with their true feelings, their true *maleness*. This was considered tremendously therapeutic for these men, getting away and having time to find their inner child, blah, blah, blah.

(I would like to point out that despite all the hype and news articles and TV stories about these *Iron John* weekends, I have never met *one guy* who went to one or even read the book. We were all too busy putting Armor All on our tires that weekend.)

If a guy came to me and said he needed to find the warrior deep inside him, to come to grips with what it means to be a *man*, this is what I would advise him.

Go cut your lawn.

Mowing the lawn is one of the last refuges for '90s-type men in search of themselves. It is also one of the few areas where we can show that we are still useful, where we can gain a sense of accomplishment. At least until our wives get the number of a reliable lawn service.

This coming weekend, I will cut my grass. I'm looking forward to it. Cutting grass carries a high job-satisfaction rating. Men can spend hours at their regular jobs without being able to look back and say: "There, I did that. There's something I achieved."

But in grass cutting, rewards are immediate. As soon as you cut that first path across the yard and look back, you see the results. A beautiful, dead-straight, foot-and-a-half path of magnificently mani-cured lawn. And before long there's another one. And another. This is the beauty of cutting the grass. This is just when you'd like to have your annual performance review done.

And not only that, mowing the lawn is relatively easy to catch on to. The rules are quite simple.

1. Pinpoint the areas of tall grass.
2. Cut them down.

While you're cutting the grass, you can get all that important thinking stuff out of the way. In fact, some of the best thinking I ever did was as a teenager, when my parents owned a ten-acre trailer park/cottage resort up near Bobcaygeon.

We had a John Deere lawn tractor, what I thought of as my own miniature green sports car with a humongous sunroof. I operated this tractor in the same manner as one of those creepy-crawly pool cleaners that wander aimlessly until all the dirt is gone. I would drive my trac-tor in a random, hit-or-miss pattern until all the grass was cut, or, when the blades were especially dull, at least beaten to death. And I would do my heavy-duty thinking, like coming up with the perfect line to convince Susan Bloomhickey to go out with me. If I did this hard enough, I wouldn't even notice the terrible noise that ensues when you get the blades stuck on a low tree stump.

Even today, I do some of my best ruminating while cutting the grass. I can compose the better part of a column while doing the front yard alone, which accounts for my unusually high overtime claim for last Saturday.

One final thing to remember: Real men don't use electric lawn-mowers. The only real lawnmower is one that uses gas, makes a huge racket, and belches all manner of toxic exhaust over the begonias and into the atmosphere. This will all change, of course, when they finally come out with the much-anticipated nuclear-powered lawnmower. If you thought disposing of grass clippings was a pain, wait until you have to get rid of the Lawn Boy's radioactive waste.

Hark! The roar of the leaf blower heralds fall

When the leaves start to change colour and drop to the ground, it's time to get all the answers to your questions about autumn chores with *Just Ask Leif*.

Today we're taking a look at the hand-held leaf blower, which has become an essential home hardware item, even if you do not have trees (see below).

Dear Leif: I work up in the traffic control tower at Pearson, and we have a continuing noise problem at the airport, particularly on weekends, when we can't hear the planes coming in because of all the leaf blowers in Bramalea and Mississauga. Some of our pilots, as they approach, say they are unable to hear our flight-path instructions. What are we to do?

— Terrified in the Tower

Dear Terrified: We are sick and tired of hearing these kinds of complaints. If you don't like the noise, you shouldn't have put your airport so close to residential neighbourhoods.

Dear Leif: We were at the theatre the other night, and right in the middle of the second act, some guy in the third row started up his leaf blower, making it impossible for me to hear whether my cell phone was ringing. I thought this was very inconsiderate. Should I have said something to the manager?

— Peeved in Pickering

Dear Peeved: Most people should know by now that using a leaf blower during a show, unless it's something like dance where there's no dialogue, is the height of ignorance. Once one person starts doing it, everyone's firing up their machines. Have these louts not heard of intermission? You should have called the manager, right from your seat with your cell phone.

Dear Leif: I love the convenience of my leaf blower, but get very nostalgic for the old days, when people would rake their leaves into the ditch and set them ablaze. Whenever I drive by a raging house fire and see smoke billowing into the air, it takes me back to my youth when I couldn't see across our street for burning leaves. How can I get that feeling back?

— *Burning Up in Burlington*

Dear Burning: You might want to check out the new Craftsman Flame-Thro Leaf Blower from Sears, which fries dead leaves to a crisp, then blows the ashes to the curbside. Also great for melting driveway ice and starting barbecues, this is truly a year-round household appliance.

Dear Leif: I don't have any trees. In fact, I live in a twenty-fifth floor condo, but I just gotta get me a leaf blower. How do I justify this purchase to my wife?

— *Eager in Etobicoke*

Dear Eager: Once you've held this baby up to dry her hair, you won't have to convince her any further of this machine's usefulness and versatility, unless, of course, you opted for the Sears Flame-Thro model (see above).

Dear Leif: I was blowing leaves off the drive the other morning and there was one, lone, damp, stubborn oak leaf that refused to budge. I aimed the machine full-throttle at this sucker for an hour. Any suggestions?

— *Dumb as a Shoe in Downsview*

Dear Dumb: If you have a garage in which to store it, you might want to consider the Mastercraft Home Backhoe from Canadian Tire.

Dear Leif: My neighbour is blowing onto my lawn the leaves I blew onto his lawn. I've tried blowing them back again, but he's bought a 232-horsepower fuel-injected turbocharged number, and I'm losing the battle with my electric model.

— *Wimpy in Waterloo*

Dear Wimpy: There's no room in this game for weenies with electric leaf blowers. Either trade up or move to Saskatchewan.

Dear Leif: What's a rake?

— *Forgetful in Flesherton*

Dear Forgetful: This is a quaint, old-fashioned term for a scoundrel, a bounder, a dissolute person, someone of disreputable character.

These two handymen are really short a loaf

If my friend Bob and I ever opened a plumbing and electrical business, I don't think we could expect to receive the blessing of the local Better Business Bureau.

Take Bob's skills at plumbing, for example. The other day, he had to run some new piping up to a bathroom fixture. This involved soldering one piece of copper pipe to another.

"As you know," Bob later explained to me, "if there's any water left in the pipe, it won't get hot enough when you've got the torch on it for the solder to melt in and make a watertight connection."

I actually knew this. As a teenager, when I worked at my family's cottage resort and trailer park, we had pipes bursting all the time. I had to do all the repairs. Of course, the fact that I was the one doing these repairs probably accounted, in no small way, for the continuing problem of bursting pipes.

Anyway, what I didn't know about was a special technique to temporarily keep water, even after you've turned it off, from trickling into the pipe. Bob had used this technique, which he'd learned from his father.

"What you do is," he said, "you stuff a little bit of bread into the pipe, which acts as a dam just long enough for you to solder the connection."

"That's a brilliant idea," I said. "Did it work?"

"Oh, yeah, the pipes went together beautifully. Only problem is, I can't get any water out of the tap now because the line's blocked with bread."

Bob figured that in his dad's day, all they had was white bread, which dissolved away to nothing. Bob had used whole grain or oat bran or something, which he figures will never break down.

Now, on to my electrical prowess.

A while back, I installed a new light in the furnace room, which necessitated moving a wire that was tacked to a beam in the unfinished ceiling.

The bracket, basically a nail shaped like a "U," was removed successfully. I shifted the wire over, and then proceeded to hammer the bracket back in place. In the process, I nicked the wire's insulation.

This produced a reaction that prompted me to phone Bob, who, while perhaps lacking some expertise in the proper use of baked goods in household water systems, could probably rewire the Toronto traffic light system in an afternoon.

With a cordless phone tucked into the crook of my neck, I said to him: "Now, I don't know everything there is to know about electrical work, but I'm guessing that if you hear a loud bang and see a bright spark, that's not good. Am I right?"

After Bob finished lecturing me about turning off circuit breakers and making me swear that I would never, *ever*, tackle another electrical project, he asked for some details of what happened.

"Well," I said, "I'm looking up at the wire now, and, hang on, I'm just moving it so I can see where the nail went in and —"

And the line went dead.

"Oh darn," I said, realizing I'd turned my head in such a way as to depress the "off" button on the cordless phone, still tucked into my neck.

"I guess I better call him back," I thought, and keyed in Bob's number several times, always getting a busy signal. Sheesh! And then the phone in my hand rang.

"Yeah?" I said.

"Are you all right?" Bob shouted. "You just about gave me a heart attack! I was ten seconds away from calling 911!"

Now, even though Bob can brag that he never made a pipe spark, and I've never stuffed an electrical socket with Texas Toast, it would probably be best if we didn't give up our day jobs.

Those Creepy Guests Who Just
Won't Leave

I spin a web of deceit

In the springtime, we go through a few seasonal adjustments at our house. These have nothing to do with unemployment or interest rates. But they have everything to do with the annual emergence of things creepy-crawly.

Every year, Spencer and Paige must reacquaint themselves with spiders and overcome their fear of them. By July, they're Arachnid Terminators, but for the month of May, and probably the first week of June, I am the assigned hit man.

One morning, Spencer came up to the kitchen, still in his pyjamas, his hair heading in easterly and westerly directions simultaneously, and said: "Dad, there's a spider in my room."

"So get it," I said.

"Daaaaaaaddddd, he's THIS big." Spencer made a circle with his thumb and index finger. The tips were a good inch from touching. Dear God, this couldn't be a spider. It must be an eight-legged hamster.

I trudged on down to his bedroom, tissue in hand. There, up where the ceiling meets the wall, right over his top bunk, was the monster, about half the size of a baby-toenail.

"Oh, for heaven's sake," I said. "Can't you get it?"

"I can't do the squishing part," he said, "when you get him in the Kleenex."

I climbed up the ladder to the top bunk, with Spencer and Paige as my audience, to corner this beast.

Corralling a spider over a bed is one of the trickiest tasks any parent will ever be asked to perform. There's a right way to perform this and a wrong way. I will explain the latter, since it is the method with which I am most familiar.

Here's what you do. When you have the spider trapped under the tissue, slowly close in on it for The Big Squish, then, as you pull the tissue away from the ceiling, allow the spider to fall out, completely unscathed.

Make sure it falls right on your child's bed. Your child's *unmade* bed.

This will produce the kinds of screams normally reserved for the most horrendous of childhood traumas, like being asked to put on clean pants to go to the mall.

The spider will quickly scurry under the covers. Pull them back, if you wish, but you will not find it. The odds are totally against you.

"GET HIM! GET HIM!" your child will ask calmly.

Once you've pulled the covers down to the foot of the bed, still unable to find the spider, you will start stripping it. Blankets, sheets, mattress pad. In seconds there will be enough linens on the floor to hold a white sale at The Bay. There will be no sign of the spider.

Your child will say: "That means he's still in here. I'm never sleeping in here again till you find it."

You have two choices, assuming you don't relish the thought of your child tucking in between you and your spouse until he's off to college. If you're a devoted, loving parent willing to make any sacrifice for your child no matter how long it takes, you will tear that room apart like you're trying to find your car keys.

But if you're a sneaky, corner-cutting, survival-minded type of parent, you will grab another tissue, shriek "There it is!" and pounce with all your fury on a piece of sock fluff. This must be accomplished with the greatest of speed and the tissue dispatched immediately before anyone gets curious enough to ask to see the evidence.

I leave it to you to guess which approach I took.

Anyway, a few days later Paige squealed that there was a spider on the rug in her room, and actually stayed there to point it out for me, instead of moving in with one of her friends. This is what's viewed around our house as progress.

Try the "Nuke 'Em" mousetrap

Welcome to our complete guide on what to do if you think you have mice:

- **Can you ignore the problem?** You're having a quiet chat with your spouse late one night in the kitchen, and hear an ominous rustling noise from somewhere behind the cupboards. You can try putting your collective fears at ease by assuming it was just the wind rubbing the branches up against the outside of the house.

  The only trouble with this theory is a) there is no wind and b) there is no tree on that side of the house.

  There may be more clues, however, that make it impossible to deny that you're now sharing your residence with a mouse. Finding a note stuck with a magnet to the very bottom of the fridge that says "Buy more Havarti" is one of them.

- **The arsenal:** Once you're sure you have a mouse, presumably you will want to catch it. There is a variety of commercial products to consider, not the least of which is a cat.

  This is not always effective, however. Sometimes cats, rather than finding a mouse in the house and eating it, will bring a live one in from the outside to play with, or conduct experiments on. If the mouse escapes, the cat will go find another one. Pretty soon your house looks like a Disney cartoon casting call.

  If you've ruled out a cat, check the anti-mouse goodies at the hardware store. There's the standard spring-loaded mouse trap, which, when triggered, swings into action with lethal efficiency, breaking your fingers and thumb while you're still trying to bait the thing with some peanut butter.

  Glue traps are shallow trays filled with an incredibly gooey substance. You'll know you have mice if, when you check the glue trap in the morning, there are little tiny slippers left stuck in it.

  If you have a real phobia about mice, you might want to consider the new "Nuke 'Em" line of extermination products. These are excellent if you're also thinking about major home renovations and need to knock down a wall or two or twelve.

- **Should you consider poison?** Definitely not. No matter how bad things get, you should hang in there.
- **Where is the mouse getting in?** If you can figure this out, you won't get any *more* mice, at least not until those already in your house start having babies. Go outside and look around your home. See any gaps around basement windows? A crack in the foundation? An out-of-use dryer vent from when the previous owners moved the laundry room to the other side of the house? A dryer vent opening that is large enough not only to admit a mouse, but a raccoon or, perhaps, an escaped serial killer, who won't mind hiding until December, when you finally open that cupboard where you keep the Christmas dishes?

  Once you've found the opening, get someone else to seal it for you, because if *you* do it, something gross will pop out, like when that guy's head shows up in the hole in the bottom of the boat in *Jaws*.
- **What should you do with a trapped mouse?** What you should *not* do is let your daughter see it, particularly if the mouse is still alive, because she will want to nurture it back to full health and keep it as a pet, which means you'll not only still have a mouse, you'll have to spend a fortune buying mouse food, a cage, and mouse fitness club workout equipment, like exercise wheels that squeak all night long.

Helpful neighbours will tell you that no one ever has just one mouse. They will tell you that if you have one mouse, you have 376,597 mice. Promise them that when you catch all these mice, you will put them in their pants.

Some eateries attract the wrong clientele

A few of the squirrels on our street have gotten together to honour Neetha as Human of the Year.

You'd think she'd be thrilled. After all, this isn't even an award for which she'd actively campaigned. I'd have been thrilled just to have been nominated, but here Neetha is, coming out with the top honour, and it's like she doesn't even care. I'd go so far as to say she's just plain ticked.

This may have a lot to do with the fact that Neetha's getting a major hate-on for these squirrels. They are messing with her bird feeder.

Ever since Neetha decided to hang a feeder from a tree in the backyard, we've had the best-fed squirrels in the neighbourhood. They've never been happier. They've certainly never looked healthier. And now they just want to show their appreciation.

Not surprisingly, some of them even appear to be putting on a bit of weight. Any day now, Richard Simmons will be dropping by, getting them started on the deal-a-meal program.

I'd never seen a spare tire on a squirrel until Neetha started having to reload the feeder on a daily basis. At first we thought we had pterodactyls, the stuff was moving so fast. But then we saw the squirrels, leaning up against the tree trunks, dabbing their mouths with tiny little napkins, sometimes taking an Alka-Seltzer, having an after-dinner cigar.

Every day we watch them, their tails twitching to and fro in the air, as they work their snouts into nooks and crannies supposedly reachable only by the narrowest of beaks. Their tiny paws manipulate the feeders, lift lids, scrape out the seed, and spread it all over the ground below.

One can't help but marvel at their initiative, their inventiveness, the sheer artistry with which they pursue the task at hand. In fact, the other day, Neetha, standing at the window observing all this, commented: "You stupid squirrels!"

It's just that Neetha was really looking forward to hanging a feeder out back so that we could all get a better look at the cardinals and jays and finches and other beautiful birds that nest in the neighbourhood.

Once she'd loaded it with seed, she waited for the birds to arrive. I quickly suspected there might be a problem, however, when the first customer did not appear in our bird book, considering that it was covered in black fur and did not have wings.

The book is *Eastern Birds: An Audubon Handbook*. We keep it on a table by the window that looks out on the feeder. It's a great help in identifying the birds that drop by. But what I'd really like to know is whether the Audubon folks have a guide to squirrels, so we could differentiate between all the dozens of bushy-tailed visitors.

Simple names would do. Something like Newman, perhaps, for the fat, lazy squirrel who hangs around on the ground waiting for the others to drop stuff down to him. Or The Amazing Francine, who hangs precariously from a branch by her hind legs while she finds a way to deactivate the Chubb security system Neetha recently installed.

Actually, she did take a trip over to the birders store for some advice, so they sold her a second feeder, this one designed to thwart even squirrels with engineering degrees, so, as you might expect, the little critters are now getting *twice* as much food as before. (I think this is when Neetha clinched the award.)

And they especially seem to love the peppery additive that's supposed to make the bird feed unappetizing to squirrels. I think they've got it into their heads that they're dining out on Cajun.

I don't know how to advise Neetha. This is the risk you take when you open an eatery. Sometimes you just attract the wrong clientele.

My "outdoor fridge" idea is a stinker

From the files of a stupid city person:

Neetha made up a pot of chili to take to the cottage. It was a good-sized pot, chock-full of the requisite 900,000 kidney beans. We were having guests for dinner, and up north, where there's lots of wide open spaces and fresh air, chili is a safe thing to serve.

Neetha made a lot because our guests have the same philosophy about special dinners as we do: stuff your face until it hurts. No meal is really a success unless you've been moved away from the table on a four-by-eight sheet of plywood, moaning about how maybe you should have passed up the third slice of pie.

But the amazing thing was, after we'd finished, there was still half a pot of chili left.

And there was the dilemma.

Our refrigerator was the kind you see in most cottages. Manufactured several hundred years ago, it's a big, squat thing roughly the size of a VIA diesel, yet it has no more space in it than a Honda Civic glove compartment.

It will hold a carton of milk and a ham sandwich, unbuttered.

Where were we to store this chili?

"No problem," I said. It was the fall, and the overnight temperatures were dropping to only a few degrees above freezing. "We have the world's biggest fridge outside."

"You can't just leave it outside," Neetha cautioned.

"Well, of *course* not," I said. "I'll wrap it tight in a garbage bag, wind the top around a few times and set it on the step just outside the door."

Neetha looked unconvinced. "Don't you think it would be better to put it in the shed?"

I shook my head. "It'll be fine." I, after all, spent years living in the country as a teenager before moving back to the city, and knew about these things.

I put the lid on the chili pot, tucked the whole thing into a green bag, wound it up tight — hermetically sealed, really — and before we went to bed, set it into the cold night air just by the door.

It was about 2 a.m. when we heard the THUNK!

Neetha and I sat bolt upright in bed. "My god," she said. "The chili."

We ran to the door, jammed our heads together to look out the window, and flicked on the light.

It was easily the biggest skunk I'd ever seen. Among his associates, he would be The Head Stink. And we couldn't even see all of him. His head and paws were well into the green garbage bag, which had been dragged down two steps, the chili pot still inside.

Neetha said something. I think it may have begun: "I told you . . ." Attempts to flatter her — after all, here was one more she could add to her list of chili admirers — were fruitless.

The skunk was feasting quite vigorously. I began flicking the light on and off to scare him away. Neetha banged on the door.

Then it hit us. *What on earth were we doing*?

The last thing we wanted to do was tick him off in the middle of dinner. And suppose we could scare him off? Would we rush out and save the bit of chili he hadn't devoured? Which of our friends would we serve *that* to?

The next morning we surveyed the damage. Neetha looked at me. I think she was wondering whether her life would have been better had she married a spark plug.

About then we were struck with a horrifying realization. We all know the trouble a regular skunk can unleash on the unsuspecting.

What about a skunk powered by half a pot of potent chili?

Be afraid. Be very afraid.

Musings on Amusement

The Entertainment System

Lust in the dust

Those of us concerned about the proliferation of sex and violence in mainstream entertainment sure can be grateful for the efforts of the American Life League, a so-called Christian group based in Virginia.

In an age dominated by hard-core pornography, lyrics that promote violence against women, and flicks that glorify the use of guns, this group has zeroed in on the real enemy:

Disney

Yes, the American Life League has found all kinds of subliminal sexual messages in Disney animated features. When viewing *The Lion King* frame by frame, they say, the word SEX can be seen for a millisecond in some dust that's stirred up when the character Simba flops down on the edge of a cliff.

Judie Brown, the group's president, said in a Reuters News Agency story: "A lot of young mothers are very, very upset."

I should think so. There's no doubt in my mind that children are going to grow up with some pretty twisted notions about sexuality if their parents are up night and day going through cartoon videotapes a frame at a time hunting for the naughty bits.

Some of the fallout from this righteous indignation has been to make *The Lion King* more of a family movie than ever before. At our house, we hadn't watched the movie in months, but after the American Life League's attack, our whole family sat riveted in front of the set as we went through our copy of the video, searching for that offensive dust cloud.

And then, suddenly, there it was! The grown-up Simba flopped down on the cliff's edge, sending some dusty particles swirling up into the night sky.

Using the VCR remote, we froze the dust, then advanced the movie a frame at a time.

The dust particles appeared to be forming letters. Was that an S? Did we see an E? Were those little sparkly dots at the end forming an X?

It sure looked like it, although the penmanship was pretty shabby. I began to wonder if some of Disney's animators were former doctors. Anyway, once we had this image frozen, all we had to do was squint a little and kick our imaginations into overdrive.

Now that I've seen the word SEX in *The Lion King*, I understand the American Life League's concerns. Now, every time I see a cloud of dust, my thoughts turn positively lustful. Soon, marriage counsellors trying to put the spark back into troubled couples' lives will advise them to throw out their dustcloths.

I wish we had the American Life League's moral guidance up here in Canada. This week we've been bombarded with the word SEX in our household. The kids are coming home with all kinds of school forms, for insurance, after-class programs, you name it, and many of them include the following:

"Sex: M or F?"

Why we allow young minds to be polluted in such a fashion in the public school system is nothing short of a national scandal.

Martha's much scarier than Mulder

Tonight promises to be very scary at our house.

You might think this is because this is the night we've all been waiting for, the follow-up to last season's cliffhanger on *The X-Files*. We're desperate to find out what's happened to alien hunter Fox Mulder, last seen discovering an underground boxcar filled with icky alien skeletons, moments before the evil government cover-up artists blast it with their flamethrowers.

But the return of this spooky sci-fi show is not necessarily what makes tonight so frightening. It has more to do with the fact that, well, not exactly all of us are looking forward to the season premiere.

Paige wants no part of it.

She doesn't want to tune in to *The X-Files*. She doesn't care what's happened to Mulder, or whether his partner, Scully, will be stripped of her FBI credentials. It matters not one iota to her whether they'll find definitive proof of life from other galaxies.

She doesn't even want to hear about *The X-Files*, and that includes having to listen to Spencer rehash the previous night's episode over breakfast. (Nothing goes with a bowl of corn flakes quite like an explanation of how you can contract unsightly lesions through alien encounters.)

X-Files night is traditionally reserved around here for plopping down in front of the tube. It's the only activity anyone has the energy for, plus it's the only night of the week not filled with karate or ballet or math or swimming lessons or parent–teacher interviews or hurried trips to the store to bring in enough groceries to keep us alive for a few more days.

A couple of years ago, when it was still broadcast on Friday nights, Spencer and I discovered *The X-Files*, and before long Neetha was getting interested as well.

But after happening to catch part of an episode where heroes Scully and Mulder grow old on a ghost ship, Paige couldn't get to sleep that night. There was no need to tell her that from here on she couldn't watch the show if it scared her that much; she immediately set that rule for herself.

So now, when that familiar theme music kicks in at 9 p.m., you can expect to hear from some corner of the house: "TURN THAT DOWN!"

Paige has learned to cope quite well while the rest of the family abandons her. Sometimes she snuggles into the corner of her bed and reads the latest Baby-sitters Club book, or Roald Dahl's *Revolting*

Rhymes. I fear she may join up with one of those literacy groups, made up of concerned children trying to convince their parents of the importance of reading.

But other times Paige will closet herself in our bedroom, where she can't hear the TV from the family room, and watch something on the tube in there. Often it's one of those mindless ABC sitcoms, like *Step by Step*, which not only stars Suzanne Somers, but gives every indication of being written by someone equally talented.

But, flipping through the dial, Paige has come across, on the Life channel, *Martha Stewart Living* and *Lynette Jennings Home*. She *loves* these shows. She can learn how to start an herb garden! Make a weather vane! Turn that plain room into something fancy with a chair rail and some wallpaper! It's so easy when you know how!

This carries her right through to when we finish watching *The X-Files*.

Now, watching Mulder and Scully track down evidence of alien abductions may be scary, but that's nothing compared to a young girl who wants to make beeswax candles and sponge-paint her room at 10 p.m.

Encore! Encore! NOT!

President Clinton's new rule that all televisions in the United States be equipped with a "V-chip" is fine by me, but there are other areas regarding children and entertainment appliances that need addressing.

Sure, being able to program your television so that your kids can't tune in violent shows will be welcomed by parents, but we also urgently need technological changes in the field of audio electronics.

Specifically, I'd like to see all compact disc players equipped with an "R-chip" that would make it impossible for songs to be repeated endlessly.

Let me explain.

The Entertainment System

Paige has a small desktop CD player in her bedroom and a modest CD collection. She's graduated from the traditional kiddie fare (Fred Penner, *The Little Mermaid*) to more contemporary tastes.

She wants the music she hears on the car radio, which, if she's sitting in the front seat, she likes to turn up, so as to drown out any annoying interruptions from sirens, car horns, earthquakes, or paternal pleadings that her father's teeth have started to rattle loose.

When she's in her room doing whatever it is little girls do in their rooms (there are some things I'm not allowed to know), she likes to play her music. So she puts on Des'ree, or Sheryl Crow, or Mariah Carey, or Ace of Base, or The Spice Girls.

This is, for the most part, pretty good music. At least it's not pretty *awful* music. We can be grateful we haven't heard "At the Copa, Copacabana" coming from Paige's room. So I generally don't mind when I'm doing some work next door in the study, listening to her discs playing in the background.

But after a while, I get the vague feeling I'm in a time warp, that things are repeating themselves. I have been listening to "You gotta be bad/You gotta be bold/You gotta be wiser" and I am thinking, you gotta be kidding. I've been listening to this Des'ree hit for longer than it takes Pauly Shore to get an Academy Award nomination.

But that's not all. Does "The Sign" by Ace of Base take up more time than an Oliver Stone movie? Can it be that Sheryl Crow's "Can't Cry Anymore" stretches out longer than a morning commute when nine lanes are being merged into one?

I decide to investigate, poking my head into Paige's room. "Honey, haven't we been hearing this tune for quite some time now?"

"I LOVE this song," she explains.

I look at her CD player. There appears, on the small digital readout that tells you which track is playing, a small word: "Repeat." And it is activated by pressing a button labelled: "Repeat."

"Have you heard any of the other songs on this CD?" I inquire.

"No," Paige says. "I really like THIS song. All you have to do is press that button and you get to hear it all the time."

And so it goes. The same tune, playing over and over again, until you realize it's become permanently etched into your brain, jammed in between the McDonald's "Have you had your break today" jingle and "Masquerade," that song from *Phantom of the Opera* that always sets my teeth on edge.

This is why I've concluded that what parents need, every bit as much as a "V-chip," is an "R-chip" that will deactivate a CD player's Repeat button in such a way that it can't be countermanded by a child.

We can't wait for the United States to set new rules. We have to lead the way. Before Paige discovers heavy metal.

My movie-rating system

What this province needs, especially during the Christmas season, is a new rating system for movies.

The method currently used, with G, PG, PG-13, AA, and R, just isn't good enough. Oh sure, it's helpful to know that *Pulp Fiction* is rated R and that it might not be the best thing to take your kiddoes to, what with hypodermic needles being plunged into people's chests and a car wash scene that is very far removed from anything that's happened in your own driveway.

But the Ontario Film Review Board needs to go a little further. It needs to adopt a version of the Barclay Movie Rating System.

It's very straightforward. Is the new blockbuster children's movie coming to a theatre near us a One-Parent Movie, or a Two-Parent Movie?

Some background.

Neetha and I regularly drag Spencer and Paige to the movies. This is largely because Neetha and I have always loved to go to the show. Now we're sharing that passion with our children.

We've molded these kids into good moviegoers. They pay attention, they keep questions to a minimum, they don't run up and down the aisles. Spencer reaches too often into my popcorn bag, but that's about it.

When we go as a family, we try to find something the parents can tolerate, if not outright enjoy. Disney flicks, sci-fi, moderately intelligent comedies, Indiana Jones–type stuff. These are two-parent movies.

Sometimes, though, a flick comes along that the kids are dying to see but the parents are not. *Super Mario Brothers, Cop and a Half, Dumb and Dumber, Ace Ventura, Pet Detective.* The list goes on. These are one-parent movies.

These movies have been shown in laboratory tests to destroy millions of parental brain cells. The Siskel–Ebert experiments, conducted in Chicago in 1987, found that parents exposed to too many of these kinds of movies lost the ability to tell Anthony Hopkins from Adam Sandler.

It's criminal enough that one parent must endure these flicks in a supervisory capacity. But to drag in *two* adults surely violates several provisions of the Geneva Convention.

So when an acceptable-yet-terrible movie comes along that Spencer and Paige want to see, Neetha and I must negotiate who will take them.

"*Dumb and Dumber,*" Neetha may say. "That sounds like one you might enjoy."

I might go along with this, if only it might get me out of *Little Women.* Not only does this look like a one-parent movie (and it's not going to be me), but it also has all the earmarks of a one-child movie. I can tell you right now that there's no way, *nohow,* that Spencer is going to be talked into seeing a movie called *Little Women,* unless it's a new version of the Louisa May Alcott story subtitled: "See How Alien Mutations Shrink Earth's Females to Half Their Normal Size!"

Neetha has said it wouldn't hurt Spencer, and it wouldn't hurt his *father,* to see a movie featuring a strong female character. So we have promised to rush right out and rent *Aliens* again, so we can watch Sigourney Weaver kick some outer space butt.

While the film review board is considering my proposal, they might also expand on those little blurbs that accompany ratings, like "Brutal Violence" and "Sexual Situations." They could add things like "Mind-numbing Stupidity" and "Will Make Parents Lose Will to Live."

Finally, for movies so stupid even children shouldn't see them, I propose the Double R Rating, which would stand for Really Restricted. These would be no-parent, no-child movies to which no one would be admitted while the film was in progress.

I have seen Hell, and it's a video store

Hell is a video store.

I used to think it was the mall, but I've changed my mind. When your life ends and the guy in charge says, "No, I'm sorry, but you're taking the DOWN elevator," the doors will not open on caverns of fire and your tour guide will not be a gent with a pointed tail. Instead, they'll open on a mega-size video store, and you'll be assigned two children who would rather fight to the death than agree on which movie to rent for that evening's entertainment.

I take you back now to last week. Spencer and Paige have finished school, and there's no better way to celebrate not having to get up early in the morning than staying up late watching a rented movie.

This is the plan. Neetha and I are getting one movie for us, to watch upstairs, and the kids are going to get one for themselves, to view in the basement. (I know, I know, a two-VCR family. It's absolutely disgusting. But you should know that firing up the kids' VCR, a coal-burning model, always requires hitting the Play button ten or twelve times and is much like trying to turn over a 1976 Capri I once owned.)

Right away, Neetha and I settle on *Heavenly Creatures*, which may sound like a steamy adult flick, but is actually the true story of two teenage girls in New Zealand who commit a murder in the 1950s.

Now all we have to do is find something for the kids.

But here's the problem. Spencer and Paige not only have different tastes, but because he's three years older, there are some flicks we think he *might* be ready for but are pretty sure she isn't, and some movies

she'd love that would induce a case of dry heaves in Spencer. She's reaching for *Black Beauty* and he's running to the counter with *Teenage Mutant Heart Chompers.*

"Hey, look," I say, voice full of enthusiasm, grabbing a new release, *Far from Home*, the boy-finds-dog, boy-and-dog-get-lost, boy-and-dog-survive movie. (I hope I haven't ruined it for you.) Both kids frown. This is the *other* problem. They can spot a "family-feel-good" movie a mile away. If the jacket blurbs say "Enriching!" or "Heart-warming!" or "A delight for all ages!" they say, in unison: "Pass!"

(When you see this kind of cynicism in children so young you can't help but feel there's hope for the future.)

Anyway, Spencer grabs the box for *The Shadow*, the Alec Baldwin flop. "Paige, read this. It looks awesome."

She scans the write-up. "No," she says dismissively. "As soon as I see the word 'superhero' I KNOW it's going to be stupid. Mom, what about *Earth Girls Are Easy?*"

"Hey!" Neetha says, on our fifth pass down the "New Releases" rack. "*Camp Nowhere.*"

"Seen it."

"Seen it."

Getting desperate now: "Would you like to see it again?" And the kids demonstrate their skill at the newly sanctioned Olympic event, synchronized eye-rolling.

"Oh!" Spencer cries. "*Scanners!*" The box for this pictures body parts in various stages of becoming disconnected from each other.

"Not a chance," we say.

Finally, we suggest (perhaps plead would be more accurate) the funny *and* more-or-less appropriate Steve Martin–Lily Tomlin comedy, *All of Me.*

But just when I think this has all been sorted out, Paige says, "Hey, Dad, how 'bout this?"

I look at the box. "No," I say, "you cannot get *Cannibal Hookers.*"

Losing Our Way in the World

The Getaway Car

Rules for Disney World

If you're a parent, skip this. This one is for your kids.

Spencer and Paige have just returned from a week at Walt Disney World, and have prepared a thorough list of secret tips for you boys and girls out there whose parents have lost all their faculties and are considering taking you to Florida.

This simple guide will ensure that your trip to the Magic Kingdom is one you'll always remember, and one that your parents will be unable to forget, even with therapy.

- Always run ahead. You can't control your excitement. Break free of your parents' grasp and dart through thick crowds so Mom and Dad have brief but intense anxiety attacks that will take their minds off their overheated and swollen feet.
- At the hotel breakfast, tell your parents you're starved. No wimpy $2.99 items off the kiddie menu. You deserve the $6.95 *adult* breakfast buffet, because you're walking all day, and *need* it.

  Persuade them you can eat twelve muffins, sixteen eggs, nine pieces of toast, and four pounds of bacon. You'll skip lunch. Once your parents agree, and have indicated to the waitress that they will, in fact, pay the full adult rate for you, eat one peach slice and a couple of home fries, and announce that you're full.
- *Never* use sidewalks. They are for parents. Jump up and walk along the sides of retaining walls, plants, bridge railings, or curbs. Fall into gardens.

  At the airport, climb onto the heat vents and use them as

sidewalks. Walk backwards on the people mover so you get nowhere.

- Also at the airport, when your parents are saddled down with three suitcases each, your dad is fumbling for his wallet, and your mom is trying to find the plane tickets in her purse, hand them your hat and ask them to carry it. Better yet, say you're tired and ask to be carried.

- Tell your parents you can handle The Unbelievably Totally Scary Wet-Your-Pants Roller Coaster, so *please* let's join the hour-long lineup for it, because you want to go on it so bad.

  After you've been in line fifty-seven minutes and are just about to get on, chicken out.

- Similarly, after your parents have stood in line at the fast-food counter long enough for your clothes to go out of style, announce just as they're placing the order that you have to go to the bathroom *right now*.

- Never, *ever*, let your parents sleep together in the hotel room. If you have a sibling, argue with him or her over who gets to sleep with Mom first. Sleep sideways.

- When the bus to the Disney-MGM Studios park slows down to allow a duck and several little ducklings to cross the road safely, go *OOOOHHHHH!* and *AAAHHHHHH!* and say that *this*, not Space Mountain, not the Indiana Jones Stunt Spectacular, not the Star Tours ride, was the very *best* thing you saw.

  Say this when your parents are talking about whether they'll have to take out a second mortgage to pay for this vacation.

- Remind your parents that by dragging you away on a surprise trip to Walt Disney World, you'll miss *X-Men* on TV.

- Eat balanced meals. For example, if you have a hot dog and fries Monday, get a *burger* and fries Tuesday. On Wednesday opt for the deep-fried *chicken fingers* and fries. And don't forget fruit! Strawberry ice cream bars are sold throughout the parks.

- You owe your parents big, so when you get home, make your bed, tidy your room, and turn out the lights the first time you're asked. But the second day back, you can let things get back to normal.

Kids: the ultimate driving hazard

You may have heard that Brazil has banned using cellular phones while driving. To my mind, this takes away most of the fun of having a car phone. The whole point of having one is to be seen using it, by other motorists, *while* you are driving, so you can show them that you are better than they are.

If you have to pull over to use it, people driving by will think: "Ha! His car broke down and now he's calling for help. Next time, buy a tune-up instead of a phone, sucker!"

Brazil is concerned that talking into a cell phone is bad, if you mean by bad that you get so distracted using the darn thing that you drive off the end of the lift bridge.

Well, maybe. But if our governments are genuinely concerned about driver distractions, there are more serious things out there than cell phones.

It's time children were banned from cars.

Of all the things that can take a driver's mind off the task at hand, it's children. Here are just three of the things you can be called upon to deal with when you have children in the car:

- Territorial disputes: These occur when one child launches a major incursion into the seating area of another. For example: "Don't you put your comic there! That's where I put MY comic! MOVE YOUR STINKING COMIC!"

  As the driver of the car, you will be drawn into negotiating some kind of settlement, often during a blinding snowstorm where you think, but are not sure, that you're crossing a 500-foot-high suspension bridge, where one false turn will send you hurtling down into the murky depths. Don't get bogged down in details of just how far the comic crossed into enemy territory. Just take a deep breath, try to be calm, and then scream: "Stop it! Stop it! STOP IT!"

- Spills: A leading factor in backseat disasters are box juices. No child can resist squeezing a box juice that has just been punctured with a straw. The child knows what's going to happen. The child knows there's going to be a mess. But the temptation is too great. "Dad! Grape juice has just squirted all over the velour upholstery!"

This tends to happen while you're tackling the on-ramp to Highway 401, trying to sneak your way in between a car-carrier loaded with vans that appear to be held on with masking tape and a truck with wobbly wheels hauling radioactive waste.

- The Fake Siren: I used to be quite good at this myself, actually. Some kids do excellent impressions of distant emergency vehicles by creating a wailing noise deep in their throats.

  If they do it too loudly, it's immediately spotted as fake, but done softly it never fails to get the driver to start checking her mirrors and looking for a place to pull over. The longer the siren persists, with the driver unable to locate its source, the more panic-stricken she's likely to become.

  A child who can reproduce convincingly the sound of metal crashing into metal can really make a parent proud.

The government can go ahead and conduct its own studies if it wants, but the evidence is already there. In fact, as long as children are allowed to ride in cars, drivers will need their cell phones to call for help.

Backseat meltdown

We're heading back from a weekend in cottage country, and are only ten minutes from home. That may not sound like a long time, but I can't get there fast enough.

We have, the four of us — Neetha and I, and in the back, Spencer and Paige — been in this car for more than two hours. It's no marathon drive from Orlando, but it is, on this Sunday evening, *enough*.

For the last half hour I've been acutely aware of Neetha's behaviour. She has been crossing her legs. She has been putting her feet up on the dashboard. She has been fiddling with the radio buttons, slapping her hands on her knees, rolling her head around on her shoulders. She has tried to pull a hair on *my* leg.

She is going nuts.

"I've got the fidgets," she explains. "I HAVE to get OUT of this car."

Usually it's the kids who are restless, who must rely on that old standby method of relieving boredom: driving everyone else in the car crazy. But as it turns out, they're prepared to pull their weight, too.

Spencer announces that he is desperately in need of a trip to the facilities.

"We'll be home in another ten minutes or so," I tell him. "There's really not any place to stop. Can you make it?"

I can almost hear the gnashing of teeth from the backseat. "I THINK so," he says. But his voice lacks conviction.

"I think I'm about to explode."

This conjures up several unpleasant images. "In fact, I think I am nearing Total System Failure," Spencer says.

"I HAVE to get OUT of this car," Neetha says.

"Mom," says Paige, who is keeping herself busy with some scraps of paper, "do you have some tape?"

"Tape?" says Neetha. "Tape?"

Maybe you think the biggest failing of today's parents is they don't spend enough time with their kids. That they don't instill in them a strong sense of values. That they're too loose with discipline.

It's none of those things. Our daughter will tell you that it's the failure of parents, when taking kids for a drive in the car, to bring a full complement of arts and crafts supplies.

How can you even *think* of going out without scissors, glue, and construction paper?

"We're approaching Total Nuclear Failure," Spencer says. "Total system failure in five minutes. Evacuate the ship." And then, his naval "red alert" impression: *"UUUNNNKKK! UUUNNNNKKK! UUUNNNNKKK!"*

Paige, no longer focused on craft-making, is now singing the commercial jingle for Marineland, which, in case you didn't know, is a theme park that features, in addition to killer whales and dolphins, lots of *water*. Just the thing to take Spencer's mind off his current predicament.

"Niagara Falls, Ontario —"

Even better. The image of billions of gallons of water cascading over the Horseshoe Falls can only help Spencer forget that he'd trade all his Lego for a pit stop.

"— the place to go —"

"*UUUNNNKKK! UUUNNNKKK!* Core meltdown imminent! Are we almost home?"

"Everyone LOVES Marineland!"

"Why does she think I'm going to be carrying tape around?" Neetha asks me, putting her feet on the dash, then down. "What about bristol board? Magic markers? Perhaps a three-hole punch? Let me just check my purse."

We pull into the drive like Mel Gibson and Danny Glover arriving at a crime scene in *Lethal Weapon*, tires squealing, doors being thrown open, people running for their lives. Spencer's so anxious to get in the house it looks as though he could, were it not for the pressure it would put on his bladder, squeeze through the keyhole.

If you happen to get behind us on the highway this summer, let me give you a bit of advice. Don't even *think* of honking.

What really separates us from the United States

While on a family trip to the U.S. recently, I noticed that many of the differences between our two countries are quite subtle, although you always know when you've crossed the border, because every two seconds the interstate goes *tha-THUNK!*

These subtle signs — some of them *real* signs — are what caught my eye, like the one in a urinal in a restaurant men's room in Connecticut. The filters that keep cigarettes from clogging up the plumbing carried these words: "Don't Do Drugs."

In Canada, the most you ever see at the business end of a urinal are those pungent white hockey pucks, a kind of tip of the helmet to our national game. You don't expect a public service announcement down there. But if you've got a point to get across, there's no denying this is as effective as a roadside billboard. (If this is where they're getting the message out, Connecticut health officials must not see drug abuse as a serious problem among women.)

More alarming was the sign we saw in New York state, as we approached the Tappan Zee Bridge across the Hudson River.

"Trucks with Class A or B explosives take next exit."

This really woke me up. When you're approaching the Gardiner Expressway into Toronto, you rarely see the message: "Trucks with nuclear devices take Lake Shore."

I looked to see how many trucks were getting off, but everyone was heading towards the bridge. This meant one or more of the following:

- They were not carrying Class A or B explosives.
- They *were* carrying Class A or B explosives, but decided, what the hey, we'll steer around the potholes.
- They were merely carrying Class C, D, E, F, G, H, I, J, K, L, M, N, O, P, Q, R, S, T, U, V, W, X, Y, and Z explosives.
- It's okay to carry Class A or B explosives in your car, minivan, or school bus.

Almost any way you looked at it, I had to be surrounded by drivers hauling, on bald tires, dynamite, nitroglycerine, and imported Scud missiles.

The last time I was this unnerved by a highway sign was at a Florida toll booth, where you were gently reminded that, should you decide to rob the toll collector, there was a good chance a state employee with a high-powered rifle already had you in his sights.

Which brings me to one of the two remaining differences between us and the U.S.: guns. While we were there, the House of Representatives was overturning a ban on assault rifles, because, as New York

Republican Gerald Solomon explained, every housewife needs an Uzi.

I was reading this while having lunch at a fast-food joint, where I spotted the most constant reminder that I wasn't in Canada anymore: the individually wrapped straw. In the U.S., straws come sheathed in paper, unlike in Canada, where they are presented to consumers naked. (That's the straws, not the consumers.)

Our kids would rip off one end, then blow into the straw, propelling the rest of the wrapper into my eye.

Clearly, the U.S. food industry knows something we don't: that dreadful ailments can be contracted from using an unwrapped straw. Makes you wonder whether British cows have been drinking from them.

Ensuring that each and every straw is hermetically sealed must keep thousands of Americans busy. This could be the answer to our own unemployment problems. Ottawa should put everyone to work wrapping straws. In Ontario, it could be a workfare project.

It was a comfort while on vacation to know, once you'd reached a burger joint without being blown up by a passing tractor-trailer, that when some nutbar burst into the place wielding an Uzi, the straw you were using to suck down your milkshake was germ-free.

Could men from Mars get here without asking for directions?

Even though *Men Are from Mars, Women Are from Venus,* the book by John Gray on how the sexes interact, has been atop the bestseller lists since the invention of the telescope, it never addresses the question inherent in its title: How did those men and women get here?

After all, interplanetary travel is no easy thing. Did the men have maps? Were they so sure of themselves they figured they could find Earth by just winging it, and then when they *did* get lost, were they too proud and stubborn to stop at the closest asteroid to ask for directions?

And what about the women, coming here from Venus? Did they

take a charter? Drive themselves? Did they stop along the way several times because they were sure they should have made a left at that last pile of NASA space debris?

How men and women get where they're going has always fascinated me. In our house, the men (me and Spencer, an apprentice man) always think they know where they are, always know the shortest route to get someplace, and are unbearably smug about it.

The women, on the other hand (Neetha and Paige) don't know north from south or east from west and couldn't care less because all they have to do is stop and ask somebody for help. Most guys I know would rather go on Oprah and admit before an audience of millions that they look pretty good in heels than allow a stranger to know they have no idea where they are.

All of which brings me to this really neat gadget you may have read about recently, called the Global Positioning System (GPS for short). No bigger than a remote control (something we men-types are pretty familiar with), it can tell you, once you've simply punched in a few co-ordinates, exactly where you are in the world. We are talking the whole planet here. And it can tell you how to get where you're going, all because it's hooked up to twenty-four satellites wandering around the globe that are sending signals back and forth to your GPS.

I mentioned the existence of this gadget to Neetha, in a purely *helpful* sort of way, you understand. I explained, for example, how the co-ordinates for the CN Tower are 43 38 31 North, 79 23 12 West, and that if you're headed to Yonge and Bloor, that's 43 40 12 North, 79 23 10 West.

"Will this machine tell me," she asked, "that if I'm going to Pat's, I turn in at the drive with the little red post by that white octagonal house, four lanes past the mailbox on that post carved to look like a leprechaun?"

"Uh, no," I said, "I don't think it will do that."

"Sounds pretty useless to me," she said.

Speaking of Pat, who shares Neetha's sense of direction, the two of them went to do a little shopping one day in Buffalo. Fearing the worst, I drew them a detailed map, knowing that if I didn't, it was unlikely I'd ever see either of them again.

This is the story (or at least the part they were willing to tell me) I heard when they got back.

Despite the map, they got lost and stopped at a gas bar for directions. Pat asked the man standing behind the counter how to get to one of the outlet malls. From back of the counter, the man pointed and gave her a few helpful tips.

Pat, who was driving, hopped back into the car with Neetha, confidently put her foot to the gas, but was barely out of the parking lot when she slammed on the brakes.

"Wait a sec," she said. "Which way was that counter facing?"

So these inventors of the Global Positioning System better listen up. Forget longitude and latitude and co-ordinates. Just tell us which way the counter is facing.

In the meantime, some of the guys and I are heading back to Mars for one of those monster spaceship rallies. Don't worry, we know how to get there.

Lost in the 'burbs

I want one of those maps like they sell in Hollywood. A map to the stars' homes.

But the one I'm looking for is a little different. I need a map to the homes of my daughter's friends. Considering the mistake I made the other day, the sooner I get it, the better.

Some background first.

Since starting in a new school last September, Paige has devoted herself to the most important of academic pursuits: making friends. If this were something she could be graded on, she'd earn an A+.

Paige is always getting together with Heather or Juliann or Nicole or Lauren or Ilse or Ashley or Laura or Caitlin or Natalie or *whoever* after school and on weekends. This helps keep Neetha and me busy in our second careers, as operators of the Barclay Chauffeuring Service, as we either drop Paige off or fetch her from all ends of the neighbourhood.

One recent morning, before everyone went their separate ways, the phone rang. "It's for you," I told Paige.

She chatted for a moment on the extension in the kitchen and asked me: "Heather wants to know if I can come over to her house after school today? Her mom's going to pick us up at school and you'd have to get me at 5:30?"

"Fine," I said.

So later that same day, at 5:25 p.m., I fired up the limo and headed off to Heather's house. I'd been there before and was pretty sure I could find it again.

I turned down the street. I hadn't bothered to check the actual address before heading out. The house would be easy enough to recognize. The colour, the gardens, maybe the make of car in the driveway. There would be enough clues.

I drove up the street slowly. Not that house, not this one, not . . . Yes! Here was a house I recognized. I pulled the car into the driveway.

I knocked on the door. There's always that anxious moment for me, that maybe I *have* made a mistake, that maybe this isn't the house of Paige's friend.

But as the door slowly swung open, I felt a surge of confidence. I recognized this little girl with the black hair. This was definitely Paige's friend.

"Hi!" I said cheerily. "I'm here to pick up Paige."

Something seemed to be wrong. This youngster looked very puzzled to see me. Now, there was no question this was one of Paige's friends. She'd been over to play at our house, and I *knew* I'd picked up Paige here before.

But it was starting to dawn on me that maybe this little girl was not Heather.

This little girl was Juliann.

"Paige isn't here," she said. "She's at Heather's." She pointed down the street. I was off by four driveways.

If I could have made my getaway then, everything might have been fine. But then Juliann's mother came to the door, and I had to laugh and joke that I, sensitive and caring and *responsible* dad of the '90s, had come to the wrong house to pick up my daughter, which could only lead one to surmise that I had no idea where my daughter actually was. This is definitely the kind of reputation one wants to cultivate in the neighbourhood.

I got back in the car and went four houses south, where, to my incredible relief, Paige and Heather showed up at the door, giggling and laughing.

Once we were in the car, I told Paige of my mistake.

"You're kidding, right?" she said.

She was certainly hoping so. What kid wants her friends to know her father's so dumb, so monumentally *stupid*, as to show up at the wrong house to pick her up?

Then, the other night when Neetha and I went out to see Liam Neeson run around in a skirt in *Rob Roy*, I couldn't remember the colour of the garage door of our babysitter Angela's house. But I was only off by three driveways this time. I offer this as proof that we're not getting out enough.

Oh, the shame of it. If I can't get any better at finding my way around town, there may be no choice left but for me to become a taxi driver.

Get that vacation feeling right at home

For the seven or eight of you who don't head south for the March Break and feel pretty cheesed off about it, even if it means you can do your usual commute in three minutes and fourteen seconds instead of the standard hour and a half, there is a way for you to get that vacation feeling without leaving home.

Yes, it's true, and you can do it at a fraction of what those poor suckers spend to lounge about for a week in Florida or Mexico or the Bahamas.

When everyone else returns to work, you can be every bit as refreshed and invigorated. Follow our simple "March Break at Home Guide."

So get out the sunblock and flip-flops! The holiday fun begins now:

- To make your bathroom feel like one in a motel, put in a new shower fixture so complicated a safecracker couldn't figure out how to get the water to stay hot longer than twelve seconds.
- If you're wanting a more Mexican experience, leave some meat to thaw on your counter for a couple of days, then undercook it.
- Rent a shark for the bathtub.
- Close off all of your house except your bedroom, and bring the kids in to sleep with you. Let them jump on the bed. Encourage them to fight over what shows to watch on TV.

  Every five minutes, tell them to settle down because you're doing Epcot tomorrow. Yell at them. Threaten to go home.

  No matter how bad it gets, you are not allowed to leave the room.
- To get the airport experience, jam everyone into the car, then wait twelve hours for permission to leave the driveway because your bumpers haven't been de-iced.
- Have your spouse get up at 2 a.m. and make lots of noise outside your bedroom door. Have her shout things like "Why doesn't this key fit?" and "It costs HOW much for WHAT?"
- Pack a suitcase with all your favourite vacation clothes, birth certificates, a camera, and $1,000 in traveller's cheques, take it up to the airport, and leave it on one of the carousels.

  Come back three hours later, or long enough to guarantee the suitcase will be missing. Say: "Well, this is just PEACHY!"
- Buy sandbox sand or kitty litter (preferably unused). Sprinkle liberally in your shoes, dresser drawers, underwear. Pour some between the sheets, down near the foot of the bed.
- Get on the closest major highway and drive one hour in any

direction, turn around, and head back. Repeat. Make sure the kids have a cooler filled with box juices and only one Walkman, with dying batteries, between them. When they start begging to go to the bathroom, tell them it's only three hours to the next rest stop.

- Speaking of which, to recreate the interstate highway rest area experience, ask your local zoo for half a dozen baboons to play in your bathroom for an hour.
- Fall asleep under a sunlamp.
- Forget cereal and fruit. Have a typical roadside Yankee breakfast, with waffles the size of radials, a five-gallon can of syrup, a pound of bacon, four dozen eggs, a loaf of Texas Toast with three pounds of butter, and a pot of coffee with double cream and sugar, all for $2.99. (Kids eat free!) Now, to work it off, sit in your car for eight hours with the seatbelt as tight as it will go.
- Pay a neighbourhood kid to sneak in at night and make off with your wallet and credit cards.

If you do all these things, when you show up at work the next week, people will look at the expression on your face and say, "Boy, you must have been away!"

My cross-dressing smuggling days

I have no future as a smuggler. If you're some drug baron and are thinking I'd make a good mule, forget it.

Border crossings give me palpitations. Customs agents make me break out in a sweat. It doesn't matter that my papers are in order, that I do not have my jacket lined with counterfeit plates. When I'm asked whether I have anything to declare, I immediately begin to stammer and throw receipts.

I trace this back to what I refer to as The Girdle Incident. More about that in a minute.

The Getaway Car

Neetha and I and the kids were returning from a trip to Boston and as we got closer to Niagara Falls my hands started to grip the wheel more tightly and my breathing grew more rapid and shallow. I wondered if we had a paper bag I could breathe into.

"It's going to be okay," Neetha reassured me, fearful that as we passed the inspection booth I'd confess to the World Trade Centre bombing. "We haven't done anything wrong. We're not bringing back anything more than we're allowed."

My behaviour is certainly not an inherited trait. When I was a kid, my parents (both passed on now, and immune to prosecution) made something of a career of bringing things back from the U.S. and not declaring them. How does one explain, for example, a gleaming new Hoover in the backseat? "We never go on a trip without our vacuum in case I-90 is dusty."

I believe my customs phobia dates back to my late teens. When I was eighteen I persuaded my mother to let me borrow the family car and drive down to Ohio to see a girl with whom I was smitten. ("Smitten" is a word you don't see that often nowadays. If you are a younger reader, say, under seventy, substitute "had hots for.")

I was south of the border only two days, and did no shopping, so when I told the inspector at the Queenston–Lewiston bridge that I had nothing to declare, I was being completely truthful. I was not nervous. Why should I be? I had nothing to hide.

The inspector, however, was not convinced of my innocence. He handed me a slip of paper and pointed. "Pull up to that building and hand them this."

"Okay," I said. I wheeled the car into an angled spot and gave the paper to another inspector, who told me to get out of the car. He looked inside, searched the glove box, rooted around, then asked me to open the trunk.

"Sure," I said.

The customs agent looked around, but there wasn't much to see. Just my over-the-shoulder bag, and —

"What's this?" He had a small bag in his hand. It was a folded-over Kentucky Fried Chicken bag.

I shrugged. Had someone planted chicken bones in my car? Was I unknowingly smuggling the secret recipe? Did he think I was trying to run some slaw across the border?

He reached into the bag and pulled out — and I can still picture this so clearly — a woman's girdle. And a spool of thread and a needle.

"I confess," I said. "I'm Flip Wilson." Okay, I really said: "Uh, I guess that's my mom's." The inspector, who clearly knew more about me now than he cared to, said I could go.

Why, exactly, was my mom keeping an old girdle in a KFC bag in the trunk? Did she figure that one day, while motoring, she'd become so bored she'd want to pull over and stitch it up?

Anyway, that explains my fear of customs inspectors. And I guess you don't need to hear why I never buy chicken from the Colonel anymore.

Ridiculous Consumption and Other
Near-Death Shopping Experiences

There's some serious shopping afoot

"*GeeeEEEEEE?* Do we HAVE to?"

Perhaps you know this cry. When you're foolish enough to disturb a child in its natural habitat (on the couch, watching *Tiny Toons*, sneaking a bag of all-dressed chips) and suggest taking a trip to buy back-to-school clothes, chances are good that you'll hear this. In our house, you're more likely to hear it from the male of the species.

The female is somewhat more adaptable when it comes to excursions of this nature. Consider the following:

Neetha and I are at the shoe store with Spencer and Paige, but we're really here for Spencer. His sneakers have achieved a unique state of disrepair. The outsides of them appear more or less sound, but the insides are in the advanced stages of dry rot. We wonder if he has figured out a way to wear them inside-out. It's that, or carpenter ants.

We show this nine-year-old boy the shoes on display. "You like these?"

"I don't know. I guess."

"Well, how about these?"

"I don't know. I guess. Do I have to try them on?"

"No," we want to say, "we'll keep buying pairs on spec and taking them home and returning them until we find some that fit. We love the mall. We want to come here every day."

But we don't say this. We are '90s parents who understand the demeaning qualities of sarcasm, are concerned about our kids' self-esteem, and don't want to look bad in the eyes of the salesclerk.

I look around to make sure Paige has not wandered away. She's quite safe, checking out a pair of sandals.

"What about *these?*" we ask our son, holding up another shoe.

Spencer nods. They pass the test. They are not overly geeky. We ask the clerk for a pair in his size so he can try them on. I take another look at Paige.

She has one of the sandals in her hand and has caught the attention of the store's other clerk. Paige says: "Do you have these in size eleven and a half?" I find this interesting. Did I even know this information?

The woman has returned with Spencer's shoes, and we are all banging our heads together getting them laced up.

"Now take a walk in them to see if they're comfortable," Neetha says.

Spencer is worried he might become the first customer in history to break a pair of running shoes while trying them out in the store, so he stalks across the shop like Frankenstein's monster, making sure not to bend the soles.

"Loosen up a bit," I say. "Run in them. They are *running* shoes."

Imagine how someone might run, fleeing a velociraptor, with splints on up to his armpits.

"They feel great," he says. We're not sure whether to believe this. If he had clothespins attached to his toes, he'd say they felt fantastic if it meant we'd get out of the store sooner.

Paige has taken a seat at the far end of the store. The salesclerk has brought out several boxes and is helping this little girl try on sandals.

Paige tries on a couple of pairs, strolls about the store, admires them in the mirror, wonders if her Grade One classmates will find them "to die for," then tells the clerk the pink ones fit just fine.

Spencer clomps his way back over to us so that we can engage in the pushing-down-the-toe-of-the-shoe ritual. I have been trying to feel children's toes through the ends of shoes for years now and still have no idea what I'm doing. "Can you feel this?" we ask. Well, of course he can! Wouldn't you feel it if someone grabbed your foot and jammed a thumb through your toes?

We are convinced the shoes *are* comfortable and that Spencer really does like them, so we throw them in the box and take them to the counter, where Paige, smiling, is waiting with her eight-dollar sandals.

"Where to next?" she asks.

Some time after this, on another outing, when it became necessary to attend to Spencer's clothing needs, Neetha came to an interesting conclusion. She found that if there's anything more trying, more totally exasperating, than taking a boy to the store to buy new clothes, it's having your husband there to help.

I have to say, right from the outset, that I thought I was making a contribution. Where's it written that you can't tell whether a shirt looks good on your son just because you've let him pull it on over the one he's wearing?

We were passing by a children's clothing shop where Neetha often finds great deals for the kids. "I want to pop in here," she said.

Paige was thrilled. But Spencer and I did a remarkable job of concealing our excitement. We asked if there wasn't something else we should attend to, something more enjoyable, like father–son root canals.

"I'm looking for some things for YOU," Neetha warned Spencer, but a carrot was dangled. If he resisted conducting himself in the manner of an environmentalist in front of a bulldozer, he might earn himself a visit to the comics store.

But would there be something for me?

So we went in. Paige browsed the racks of girls' dresses, occasionally seeking out a salesclerk to see whether they had something in her size. It was the shoe store all over again.

Spencer, on the other hand, stood in a corner looking as though he were waiting for a cigarette, his blindfold, and someone to ask if he had a last request. I began wandering this store filled with tights and socks and belts and pants and dresses and not a power tool, jazz CD, Elmore Leonard novel, or model train to be found anywhere.

"How do you like this?" Neetha asked, holding out a red top for Spencer. I made the mistake of not looking sufficiently enthusiastic, which Spencer picked up on and said: "Uh, no, I hate it."

Spencer and I have this theory that if we pretend to hate everything, we'll get out of the store sooner. It has never worked.

That's because Neetha gives us The Look, the one millions of women direct to men with whom they've been foolish enough to have children. If I'm interpreting it correctly, it says, "If I left it to YOU to buy the kids' clothes, they'd still be in Huggies, so GET WITH THE PROGRAM."

So, while she combed the racks further, I took Spencer to the change room with four tops. Under his coat he wore a bulky sweatshirt. "Should I take this off?" he asked me.

"Nah," I said, tossing him a turtleneck.

He pulled it over his sweatshirt. About this time Neetha showed up and was unable to judge the turtleneck's merits, she claimed, since it appeared to be worn over that body armour Michael Keaton sported in *Batman*.

"Why on earth did you keep your other shirt on?" she asked.

"Dad told me to."

Once he had the turtleneck back on, *minus* the sweatshirt, he was asked to model it, which Spencer understands to mean stand as rigidly as possible with your arms stretched out like a scarecrow.

This all took its toll on Neetha. She said to Paige, who'd just finished filling out a credit card application, "Write this down. When we go on our trip, no way, *nohow*, will the boys be allowed to go shopping with us."

Paige nodded earnestly. "I have a pen and some paper in the car," she said.

NEVER send me to buy pantyhose

Welcome to *Advice for Married Guys*, where we dispense invaluable tips for husbands of all shapes and sizes and intellectual capacities.

Here is today's tip:

Never, and I mean *never*, buy a pair of pantyhose for your wife. It is not worth the risk.

And we are not speaking here of the usual risks one might expect to

The Mall

encounter on a mission of this kind. Of getting the wrong size, or selecting the wrong shade, or buying the brand that runs even before you get one leg into them. (Your wife, not you.)

Nor are we talking about the general discomfort men feel when considering the purchase of an item of female apparel. Most husbands would rather try to disengage a stick caught in a roaring lawnmower than have to decipher those charts on the backs of pantyhose packages, with the weight versus height charts that require you to no longer think of your wife as your beloved, but as a shaded area known only as A or B or C.

What we're talking about today is a much greater hazard. We're talking about the risk of getting arrested for shoplifting. And of personal ruination. I offer my true story in the hope that maybe just one man out there will be saved.

I was picking up a few things in the mall the other day. I had my list with me. Some of the items were for me. Some of them were for Neetha.

I picked up my stuff first at the drug mart. They included shaving cream, razors, and hayfever medication. I paid for these things and they were put into a plastic shopping bag.

Making my way through the mall, I passed a lingerie/hosiery shop and recalled that also on the list was a pair of pantyhose for Neetha.

I entered the store. One wall was lined with approximately nine billion varieties of pantyhose. The rest of the store was filled with racks and racks of the fanciest, frilliest lingerie I have ever seen. Some of these items of lingerie consisted of so many strings and straps and buckles that they must come with instruction manuals bigger than the one that tells you how to operate Windows 95.

A saleswoman, perhaps deducing by my open-mouthed look of stupefaction that I needed assistance, asked what it was, exactly, that my wife wanted. I told her, and as she headed over to the wall of hosiery, I bumped into a huge display of bra and panty sets on little hangers. To my relief, it did not go crashing to the floor.

She found what Neetha wanted and I followed her to the counter to pay for it. With my purchase in hand, I turned to leave and happened to catch a glimpse of my plastic bag, filled with razors and shaving cream and hayfever medicine, that was still clutched in my left hand.

There, hanging from the top of the bag, was a red bra and panty set.

Somehow, when I brushed by the display rack, one of the hangers had dislodged and caught on to the edge of my plastic bag. So here I was, wandering around the store, and about to wander around the rest of the mall, with a red bra and panty set dangling at my side.

I could imagine the story in the paper. "Well-respected family man and columnist arrested in lingerie theft. Denies it's for personal use. See page A4 for extremely large picture."

When I pointed out this freak occurrence to the saleswoman, she just laughed and put the lingerie back.

But if you're a guy, you won't see the humour in this. You'll see this as analogous to the story of the soldier who lives while his buddy right next to him takes the bullet.

That bra and panty set, you're thinking, could just as easily have been meant for you.

Check this out

My local supermarket has gone high-tech.

First of all, there's the bar code reader. My bologna, my potato chips, my Campbell's cream of chicken soup, everything is swept briefly over a piece of glass with a mysterious, glowing red light inside it. Sometimes it takes several sweeps. Then there is a beep. And then, on the digital readout over the cash register, it says "Pepsi Max $1.79."

It used to be you watched like a hawk as the cashier punched everything in. You waited for a mistake, ready to pounce and shout: "Ha! You just rang in $38.50 when it's really $3.85. I could have your job but I'm a nice guy and I can't for a minute explain how those Oreos got opened before I paid for them."

But you can't look over a bar code reader's shoulder for fear those red beams will bore right through your forehead, making it possible for you to receive CBC Radio on one of your back fillings.

Once they've figured out how much you owe, which is always more than the rough calculation you've done in your head because you've forgotten a box of Tide costs more than taking a family of four to the movies, you can use a debit card that can move your hard-earned cash *instantaneously* from your bank account to the pocket of the store manager.

You know when this happens, because you get a short, sharp pain in your side.

But despite all these technological advances, the single most important item in the supermarket has remained unchanged.

You know the thing I'm talking about.

I'm talking about the little bar that you place on the checkout conveyor belt that separates your stuff from *other* people's stuff.

Sometimes it's a stick of wood. Sometimes it's heavy plastic, or a piece of metal. Whatever the material, this is the single most important shopper's tool, because this is the device that says: "This stuff is MINE, that stuff is YOURS. I'm not paying for one celery stick that isn't mine, and I don't want any of your sordid stuff co-mingling with any of my stuff."

(If, when checking out, you're way back in line, there's time to look at some of the magazines, although selection is limited. More and more men are buying the groceries, but you still never find *Drill Press Monthly*, *Carburetor Digest*, or *True Life Monster Truck Adventures* at the checkout. You must make do with *Glamour*, *Woman's Day*, and *Cosmopolitan*, which does have, I must admit, some pretty interesting ads in the back, the likes of which, if your wife discovered them in any of your magazines, would require a lot of explaining.)

Anyway, when the person directly in front of me has put his or her groceries onto the checkout counter, I keep watching as they move forward. When there gets to be a gap of, say, four centimetres, that's enough room for a sausage stick, so I make my move.

With the speed of a Donovan Bailey, I reach into that little trough along the far side of the checkout counter, grab the bar, and deftly set it at the back of the other person's groceries.

And not on an angle. I set it across perfectly straight, right up snug against those foreign food items.

Sometimes the other person gets to the bar first. I consider this a personal affront. Sometimes they'll grab it even before they've completely unloaded their cart, so the instant all their things are on the conveyor belt, they can slap the bar down.

Not only is this taking territoriality to the extreme, I can't help wondering whether they think there's something wrong with *my* groceries.

Just because they've loaded up on caviar, lobster tails, and Decadent Dental Floss doesn't give them the right to sneer at my cartload of Twinkies, Cocoa Puffs, Kraft Dinner, and chicken weiners.

Our trip to the pet store is a real weeper

Neetha sticks a dog in my face.

"What about this one?" she says. "Do you feel anything? Are your eyes itching? Are you going to sneeze?"

This is the pet shop equivalent of going to an allergist and having your arm pricked thirty times. I am going nose-to-nose with canines of various descriptions to determine whether a dog exists that I can tolerate.

The pressure is on, let me tell you. Spencer and Paige, led by their mother, are dying to get a dog. There is only one thing standing in their way — their sneezy, watery-eyed father, who really *likes* dogs, who even had a couple as a kid, but who is now allergic to them and not quite prepared to wheeze to death for one.

"This is a bichon frise, they're non-allergenic," Neetha says, handing me this small bundle of white fur that looks like one of the slippers Paige got for Christmas. Even if I'm not allergic to this dog, would I want to be seen walking it on my street?

I've discussed this with my friend Bob, who understands the male need to be seen with a shepherd, or a retriever, even some ragged little mutt.

"But you don't want to be seen walking a fashion accessory," he says.

But Neetha loves the bichon, and so do the kids. They're unconcerned about my fragile male ego. Paige so wants a dog that she's written a poem about her longing. It goes like this:

I wish I had a dog
I wish I had a dog
A fluffy dog, a fluffy dog
I wish I had a dog
I wish I had a dog
I wish I had a dog

The poem is called "I Wish I Had a Dog." Even if you are like me and find most poetry pretty obscure, this one's not hard to get.

A woman in the pet store offers her opinion, "I was really allergic to dogs," she says, "but we got a bichon and I've had no trouble whatsoever."

Curious to know whether she suffered with itchy eyes and asthma as I do, I asked her what symptoms she exhibited with other dogs.

"I puffed up, got watery eyes, suffered severe bouts of depression, incurred memory loss and an inability to concentrate, and retained water."

And I am thinking that perhaps there's more going on here than just an allergy to dog hair.

The kids, who already know their chances of getting a dog tonight are slim, have been given permission to pick out two goldfish, at forty-nine cents each. For the last hour they've monopolized a salesclerk for a purchase that will earn the store less than a dollar.

"Yes, that one with the spots! NO, *wait*! The silvery one with the nice tail!"

My eyes are already starting to itch after a faceful of bichon. I want to rip my lids right off, put them on a table top, and go at them with a barbecue brush.

"I don't think it was the bichon," Neetha says. "I saw that puppy in the window with a Pekinese, so it probably had foreign dog dander on its face and that's what you're having a reaction to. I stuck a contaminated bichon in your face. Maybe you'd be better off with a Portuguese water dog."

My eyes stop watering long enough for me to pay for the goldfish and some fish food. We already have a bowl at home from our *last* episode with goldfish, which was not a pretty sight, but did much to add to the nutrients of our municipal waste system.

Once home, Spencer and Paige put the fish in the bowl and are fascinated by them for at least seven minutes, after which they run upstairs and throw stuffed animals at each other until one of them gets hurt and starts crying.

The fish have bought me a day's grace. Pressure to get a dog will resume tomorrow, especially after the kids find out I wasn't quite up front with them about how easy goldfish are to take for a walk.

Boo! Hunting for costumes is always scary

October certainly is my favourite time of the year.

It's not the fall leaves, or the bracing chill in the air. Not the early Christmas decorations.

No, I love October because it means we're here again in the costume section of Toys R Us, which next to, say, Beirut, is one of my favourite places in the whole world. The place where, every year, 17.2 percent of the nation's parents develop a persistent, nervous twitch.

This year it looked like Halloween was going to be so simple. Paige had borrowed a friend's princess costume. This was one beautiful princess costume. Lots of lace and finery, a little tiara.

We are talking primo princess here.

"I don't want to be a princess," Paige said at the dinner table.

"But you have that wonderful princess costume," we reminded her. "That spectacular, gorgeous, FREE, princess costume. A costume that we could never figure out how to make ourselves."

"But I really don't want to be a princess," she said. "I really, really, REALLY want to be a witch."

"Did we mention that it was free?" I said.

Well, isn't that just peachy, Neetha and I are thinking. This is when you really have to put your foot down as a parent. To lay it on the line for your child. That times are tough, and if you've got a princess costume, you are darn well going to be a princess, little lady.

Which doesn't exactly explain our presence in Toys R Us, looking at witches' capes, witches' hats, and witches' wigs. We caved in, that's what explains our presence in Toys R Us.

Caved in, because, for kids, Halloween is the most important event of the year. For most kids, it gets them more pumped up than Christmas.

Just ask Spencer, who is on the lookout for a new costume, too. So, now that we're here, I am giving him THE LECTURE.

"Whatever you decide to go out as," I tell him, "it will NOT require a mask that goes over your head."

He listens.

"That is because the year you went out as Batman, by the time you got to the second house you said your head was hot and you couldn't see, so you took it off. Then the next year, you wanted to be a Ninja Turtle, but by the time you were to the third house your head was hot and you said you couldn't see, so you took it off. That is why, this year, you are not getting a costume that has a mask."

He holds up a skull mask that completely covers his face.

"How about this?" he asks.

We end up going to a specialty costume shop. There is much examination of the costumes, which include everything from the cast of *Star Trek: The Next Generation* to Barts and Coneheads. This tends to make things even worse. There's too much selection. They'll be hanging mistletoe on us before we've made up our minds.

Paige decides, upon seeing a very cute whiskered mask, that she

does not want to be a princess and she does not want to be a witch. She wants to be a cat.

Spencer is hot for a different skull mask that covers up his entire head.

"I absolutely, positively promise you I will not take this off when I'm trick-or-treating," he says. "It is SO cool." Not only that, it has the added benefit of thick clear plastic where the eyes go, to guarantee that the child wearing it will be able to trip over curbs, bushes, and hollowed-out pumpkins filled with burning candles.

Neetha and I have now been at this for a couple of hours. We have travelled through rush hour from one store to the next, must go home and get some dinner on the table before we start eating Captain Picard's shirt right here in the store, and have decided we'll agree to almost anything if it will bring all this to an end.

Neetha looks at me. "Why can't you be one of those dads who sews?"

Spencer, Master Bargainer

No one ever expects to pay the ticketed price on an item at a garage sale, antique store, or second-hand shop. This isn't like going into Zellers or The Bay, where if you go over to the counter with a twenty-dollar shirt and ask if they'll take fifteen, the computers and price-checking equipment that are linked to every other store between here and Moose Jaw go into immediate cardiac arrest.

But it's different at an antique store, where maybe you can get that hundred-dollar blanket box for eighty-five or better. Or at a garage sale, which is where Paige spotted a strand of fake pearls — which she said would make her look "so beautiful" — going for the astronomical price of fifty cents. We suggested she offer the lady thirty-five, which was more in line with Paige's budget.

"Ummm," Paige said hesitantly to the woman overseeing the assorted bits of junk spread across the front yard, "would you take thirty five cents for this?"

The woman didn't look at all happy about this. Her brow furrowed, she ground her teeth together. "I really wanted fifty cents for that," she hissed. Hey, maybe they were *real* pearls? But because she thought it might look bad to haggle angrily with someone less than half her height, she let the necklace go for thirty-five cents, muttering as she slipped the change into her pocket.

None of this was lost on Spencer, when Neetha and I and the kids stopped at a shop halfway between Owen Sound and Southampton. The place was jammed with antiques, used books, bottles, and old magazines.

Spencer was hunting for used hockey cards, comics, and those three-holed plastic sheets that can hold nine cards and be slipped into a binder.

"You got any Doug Gilmours?" he asked the proprietor.

He opened a binder filled with hockey cards. "Here's some. They're twenty cents each."

Spencer thought about that. "Can you do any better?"

The shopkeeper seemed a bit taken aback. He must have thought twenty cents was a good price. Maybe because twenty cents *was* a good price. "Well, uh, fifteen cents, I guess."

Spencer nodded, licking his lips. "You got any card holders?"

The man dug out some of the plastic sheets. "Here you go. They're just a dime each."

Spencer nodded again. "Can you do any better than that?"

"Uh, well, maybe eight cents."

Neetha wanted to disappear into the back of the store. She wasn't about to interfere, nor did she want to hang around and watch. But wasn't Spencer doing exactly what we'd told them? Saving ten cents is as important to him as saving ten dollars is to us.

But fading away into the back of the store — way in the back — still seemed prudent.

"What's in the box way up there?" Spencer asked.

"Comics."

Spencer asked politely to see them. The man scrambled around for a short ladder and brought down a cardboard box. Spencer sifted through it and held up an *X-Men*.

"How much is this?"

"That's, oh, seventy-five cents."

Neetha waited for it.

"Can you do any better?"

"Uh, well, sixty cents, I guess."

The man prepared what may go down in shopping history as the most complicated bill of sale ever. Four card sheets regularly ten cents, for eight; two comics regularly seventy-five cents marked down to sixty; and so on and so on.

Once Spencer had concluded his transaction, Neetha reappeared from the back of the store with several antique plates.

"How much are these?" she asked the man.

"That would be sixteen dollars," he said, bracing.

"Sold," Neetha said.

"Yorkdale, we have a problem"

Telesat's Anik E-1 satellite, severely crippled after an unexplained breakdown, still manages to orbit the Earth, operating at about 50 percent capacity.

The Mall

This is without a doubt bad news. This means it's still working.

Many saw this breakdown as a communications catastrophe, since some 3.6 million Canadian households hooked up to cable depend on Anik for channels like CBC Newsworld, The Family Channel, and MuchMusic. Millions of subscribers faced the horrifying prospect of not being able to see such cultural riches as Madonna prancing about in lingerie with a bullfighter.

But it was an even bigger disaster than we could have imagined. The crippled Anik was unable to transmit background music to malls.

Who knew that mall music was being delivered to us through space? It conjures up images of a '50s horror flick: *Mall Music from Mars*. Communications experts were chilled when they first heard the words from 35,800 kilometres up in the sky: "Yorkdale, we have a problem."

Had we known satellites are used for this purpose, we'd never have waited on the off chance that Anik might one day blow a tube. We would have shot it down.

(The major difficulty in repairing this satellite, so vital to the livelihood of cable companies, is that the service people won't say what time of day they'll be coming. "Sometime between nine and four" is the best Telesat has been able to get out of them.)

The disturbing news, as we mentioned, is that Anik is still able to perform some of its functions. Novanet Communications Ltd. said its service, which, among other things, provides music to The Bay stores, was only out for about six hours when the system became crippled. If I'd known, I'd have gone shopping.

But I'm sure those working in the stores at the time were devastated by the interruption. Probably those people who hunt you down so they can shoot you with perfume were the first to notice. They put their hands over their ears and writhed in pain, like Captain Kirk always did when the aliens blew on some intergalactic dog whistle that only William Shatner could hear.

All the fuss we heard back in the '80s about the Star Wars strategic defence system pales in comparison with the notion that there are objects circling the globe beaming down "Muskrat Love" into places of commerce. I mean, given a choice between nuclear obliteration and having to listen to a James Last–type arrangement of Alanis Morissette's "You Oughta Know," which would you choose?

Mall music is the auditory version of nerve gas. You don't know it's happening to you until it's too late.

Husband: Hi! I'm back from the mall. Hmmmmmmmm hmmm hmmmm hmmmmmmmmmmm, hmmm hmmm hmmm.

Wife: Whadjya get?

Husband: Some lovely socket wrenches in spring colours . . . hmm hmmmmm hmm . . . and a self-adjusting electric toothbrush . . . hmmm hmmm hmmm.

Wife: What're you humming?

Husband: Humming? Was I humming something? Oh my god. They must have been playing it at the mall! It's "Close to You," by The Carpenters!

There must have been some fairly high-level discussions about the Anik's capabilities before agreement was reached to send it into orbit.

"Hello, satellite-launching people? This is Telesat, and we've got this $300 million baby we'd like you to put into orbit."

"Why?"

"Well, it'll prove a vital communications link for millions, bringing television and telephone signals to the far northern reaches of the country, keeping newspapers and radio stations up to date on breaking developments, and even authorizing credit card transactions."

"That's it?"

"Uh, it will also beam out mall music."

"Well, why didn't you say so?"

Butterfingers and a balanced universe

They say you can't get something for nothing. That nothing in life is free. You get what you pay for.

The Mall

But sometimes you really do get a break. And it can be delicious when it happens.

Spencer came into the office with me one recent Sunday. I had a couple of things to do and he was happy to tag along with Dad. But he doesn't care about seeing how the paper is put together. He doesn't want to meet the award-winning photographers. He couldn't care less about chatting up reporters who've sat down with Yeltsin and Clinton and Chrétien.

Spencer wants to visit the cafeteria.

One other time he came down here with me he ordered a club sandwich. Some toast, some meat, some cheese. You want the recipe, I'll mail it to you. Anyway, it was all he talked about when he got home.

Like most young boys, Spencer likes food. You wouldn't know, to look at him, that he eats any, but he's a machine, burning up fuel like a space shuttle leaving the launching pad. So any excursion, no matter where it's to, always includes a look at the culinary landscape.

So now we're down here again, except this is a Sunday, and the cafeteria is closed. But there is a room full of vending machines. He decides it's time for a candy bar.

There is a discussion. Malted Milk? Milky Way? Crispy Crunch?

We settle on a Butterfinger. He has never had a Butterfinger. Come to think of it, I have never had a Butterfinger.

We are going to buy a Butterfinger. And I have demanded a bite of it.

I slip the change into the machine and punch the numbered code. Through the glass window we watch the little plastic spiral coil back. The Butterfinger moves forwards, millimetring to the edge.

The suspense is excruciating. Whenever I buy a bag of chips from this machine, a little corner of the bag gets trapped and hangs there like Cary Grant clinging to some presidential nostril on Mount Rushmore in *North by Northwest*.

But that doesn't happen this time. Something magical happens.

Not one, but two, Butterfingers drop down into the tray.

The realization sinks in. We have paid for one Butterfinger. *But we have two.*

Spencer looks at me. His eyes dance. I push back the machine's metal door and pull the two candy bars out.

"One for you," I say, "and one for me."

"Can we keep it?" Spencer asks. He's been brought up with a healthy respect for other people's property, for doing the right thing.

I look around the cafeteria. There isn't a soul here. We're feeling a little guilty, but if we'd *lost* money in the machine there would have been no one to talk to, either. (If you want rationalizing, you've come to the right spot.)

"Yes," I say, shrugging. "I guess we can."

We peel back the wrappers and bite into our Butterfingers.

These are the sweetest candy bars Spencer and I have ever eaten. They could have been Crunchies. They could have been Mars bars. It wouldn't have made any difference.

Imagine how someone might look if he'd pulled off the Brink's job. The grin someone might have if he'd wheeled out everything from Fort Knox without a soul knowing. If he'd lined up three-of-a-kind on a Vegas slot machine.

That's how Spencer looked.

Somewhere else at this very moment someone is putting a loonie into a pop machine and getting nothing. Dropping change into a newspaper box and fighting to get the door open.

We got our Butterfingers. There is balance in the universe.

These Kids Are Out to Get Me

Up the Wall

Spencer rats me out

I plan to be a law-abiding citizen. I'm not stepping out of line.

It's not the police I fear.

It's my son. He'd rat me out in a second.

This is the kind of risk you run when you act like a father who thinks he knows everything. Your every move is scrutinized.

Take driving in the car. From where Spencer sits in the back, next to Paige, he has a clear view of the dashboard.

"What's the speed limit along here, Dad?" Spencer asks.

"Uh, it's sixty," I tell him.

"Then why are you going seventy kilometres?"

"Huh?"

"The speedometer says you're going seventy. So you're speeding, right?"

Paige panics. "Dad, PLEASE don't speed! I don't want you to go to jail!"

I don't think Spencer really cares whether I slow down or not. The important thing is, he's *caught* me.

Like the other day at the mall. I'm forever needling the other members of my family, particularly those of the female persuasion, about how they always lose their bearings during shopping excursions.

On one recent visit, Spencer and I split up from Neetha and Paige, but when it came time to regroup I headed off confidently, dragging Spencer along with me, to the designated rendezvous point.

"Dad," Spencer said, tugging at my sleeve, "we're supposed to go the OTHER way."

"Come on," I said, forging ahead.

But then I realized I wasn't getting any closer to the store where Neetha and Paige were. I was — and this was a very hard thing to accept — going the wrong way. And even worse: Spencer was right.

"Uh, let's go THIS way," I said, turning on my heels.

"You're LOST!" Spencer said. He could disguise neither his astonishment nor his glee. "You got LOST in the MALL!"

Sheesh. Would he be this happy if we were in Algonquin Park?

"It's not like I got lost," I protested. "It's just that for a brief moment I was unsure —"

"You got LOST!" It was like Christmas for him. How often do you get to correct a know-it-all Dad?

"Let's just make this our little secret," I said. "No need for Mom to know about —"

But he'd already spotted her in the distance and was sprinting ahead to deliver his bulletin.

Finally, last week, Neetha phoned to tell me to go ahead and start dinner without her, she'd be delayed. I'd prepared one of my finest meals, rice with chicken cooked in a tin of cream of chicken soup. (Here's the recipe: Chicken, one tin of cream of chicken soup. You might want to order my cookbook now before they're all sold out.)

I slid on the mitts, took the chicken from the oven, and removed the hot glass lid from the steaming cooking dish. I set it in the sink, where there was some cold water trickling.

The glass lid, with a resounding "*KLLERRSHHH!!!*" shattered into several hundred shards right there in the bottom of the sink. Spencer and Paige rushed over to have a look.

"The little knob you lift it with is still in one piece," Spencer said.

But then the heart of the matter hit home. His dad, that guy who's always picking at him to comb his hair and hang up his coat and put away his backpack, had goofed up *again*.

"Wait till Mom finds out you ran cold water on a hot lid," he said. "And I think it was an antique!"

"Yes," I said. "Antique Pyrex."

Around the third bite of dinner, we heard the front door open.

"Mom!" Spencer said, bolting out of his chair. "You're not gonna believe this!"

She didn't even have a chance to get her coat off.

So I'm keeping my nose clean. But Spencer'd better, too. One step out of line, boy, and I'm telling.

Paige, tax spy

I went over to the school the other day to take the kids out for lunch, and learned that my daughter may be moonlighting as a Revenue Canada auditor. More about that later.

Going out for lunch on a school day is a major treat for the kids. It means they don't have to run the risk of eating a lunch that may have been prepared by their father.

It's a stressful thing, having to sit in class all morning, wondering what horrors await you as the noon hour approaches. Will the bag be packed with tuna fish? Wasn't it enough that you got tuna on Monday, Tuesday, Wednesday, and Thursday?

Or will Dad once again fail to live up to the most basic nutritional standards? You love potato chips as much as anybody, but even you draw the line at Pringles sandwiches.

So, as a treat, we're going out. At breakfast, when this is proposed, there's a heated debate between Spencer and Paige over where we'll dine.

"Let's go to (name of repulsive fast-food place here)."

"I HATE that place. Let's go to (name of another, even MORE repulsive fast-food place here)."

"Ooooh, gross. I hate THAT place."

This is the midday version of the Friday night hunt for a place to eat.

Not to worry, I say. We can skip it if they can't agree, I've got lots of tuna.

Miraculously, an agreement is reached. We're going out for subs.

Terrific. I even have a sub card, which they stamp each time you go in, so that once you've bought 17,893 subs, which will only take you until the year 2034, you get a free one.

So just before I pick up the kids, I hunt around in my wallet for the card.

I look in the long sleeve where I keep cash and a few business cards ("Linwood Barclay, Columnist and Small Motor Repair"). When I can't find it there, I look behind my various credit cards, then where I tuck my driver's licence and other stuff.

No luck.

So I start removing things. As I take out the credit cards one by one, out fall forgotten ATM withdrawal slips (which explain why I haven't been able to balance our chequebook since the last episode of *M*A*S*H*), restaurant receipts, and my Price Club membership card, featuring a picture of me so flattering that I use it on my resume when applying for parts as escaped convicts on *America's Most Wanted*.

But there's no sub card. No big deal, we'll just pay the full fare at the sandwich shop.

While waiting to place our order, I mention to the kids that I'd thought I had a card, but couldn't find it.

"It's in your wallet, Dad," Paige says.

"No honey," I say, "I already looked."

"No, really, Dad," she persists. "It's IN your WALLET."

Before I can roll my eyes and tell her that she's wrong, she says, "Give it to me, I'll show you."

So she opens up the wallet and, you guessed it, whips out the card.

"Where did you get that?" I ask. She shows me how it had been slipped in with my business cards.

I present the stamped card to the cashier, and while enjoying my Italian salami and cheese, it hits me.

How did Paige know?

I ask. She shrugs innocently. Maybe she noticed it when she helped herself to her two-dollar allowance one day when my wallet was sitting by the bed. This is something I vaguely recall giving her permission to do.

But this business of opening my wallet, lifting cash, taking note of what else is there — this is when I begin to suspect that she's actually working for Revenue Canada.

Either that, or it's just a trick she learned from her mother.

These kisses are going to kill me

I've heard that the most likely time to have a heart attack is first thing in the morning. This puts heart attacks pretty high on the list of risky things that can happen to you around breakfast, next to burning your spouse's toast.

But meltdowns of various body parts are a small risk in our house compared to the perils of the goodbye kiss.

On this particular morning, taking place back when Spencer was nine and Paige was six, I must catch an early train and will be leaving before my wife Neetha treks off to her teaching job. There is the usual pandemonium associated with getting Spencer and Paige out of their overnight comas, into their clothes, down to breakfast, and out to catch the bus to school.

Spencer emerges from the bathroom and wanders into our room as I hurriedly put on a shirt. His hands look shiny, like they haven't been dried off, and he's reaching out to my bare stomach —

"*Ahhhhhhhh!*"

"Are my hands cold?" he asks.

I want to make my train, which is lucky for Spencer, because there's not time to devise a fitting punishment, like ice cubes down the back of his shirt. Instead, I try to get dressed and get something to eat. I pass by Paige's room on my way downstairs. She's surveying the clothes left out for her, aghast that her mother has chosen, on this warm spring day, when she has gym, shorts, a matching top, and sneakers! Imagine! Where is the party dress? The party shoes? Has Mom lost her mind?

"I'm off, sweetheart," I tell her.

"KISS! HUG!"

I slip my arm around her for a gentle squeeze and a peck on the cheek, then fly down the stairs. Spencer meets me at the door.

"KISS! HUG!"

He locks his arms around me in a backwards Heimlich manoeuvre. I attempt to move towards the door, briefcase in hand, his body dragging on mine. I give him a kiss on the forehead, attempting to pry him from me. I explain to him that I'm not going to Bolivia, that chances are excellent that I'll be home later the same day.

At last I become disentangled, blow a kiss to Neetha, who is running around look-ing for something that *should* be in her purse but is *not* in her purse, when a blood-curdling scream erupts from Paige's bedroom.

"*KIIIIIISSSSSS!!!*"

I whisper to Neetha like a true, loving father: "I already GAVE her her kiss!" I shout upstairs: "You already GOT your goodbye kiss! Remember?"

"*KIIIIIISSSSSSSSSSSS!!!!*"

Convincing her will take more time than just doing it again. I bound the stairs two at a time and find Paige sitting on the floor, her legs stretched out straight, attempting to pull on a pair of tights (looks like she's chosen the party dress after all), which are now bunched around her knees.

She offers her lips in a pucker but makes no attempt to get up. It's clear I'm expected not only to climb a flight of stairs to deliver this kiss, but to make a significant drop in altitude to plant it. So I bend over, from the waist, to give Paige her goodbye smooch.

I do not hear the standard *"smack"* of lips meeting lips. Instead, I hear *"rrriiipppp!"* from behind me. Very close behind me.

I quickly stand up and reach around. Neetha is at the door.

"What's wrong?"

"I think I ripped my pants."

"Turn around. If it's not that bad maybe you can get away with it."

I give her a view, craning my neck around to try to survey the damage myself.

"Ahh, I don't think so," she says. "But it's nice to see you getting some wear out of those briefs I got you for Christmas."

I race into the closet to look for something else to wear. Ripped pants off, other pants on, lifting up shirt to tuck it in, looking at watch —

"Ahhhhhhhh!"

"Are my hands cold?"

Life is but a scream

Paige is conducting some research at our house. She's trying to determine whether it's possible for her older brother to have a heart attack.

This research was not conducted under the strictest of laboratory conditions. It was conducted in the laundry room, from behind the door, at 8:23 a.m., as Spencer (hereafter referred to as the subject) came in to grab his coat and boots before shooting out the door to catch the bus.

The following observations were recorded:

When the researcher emitted a loud *"BOOOOO!"* from behind the door, the subject's body exhibited several responses. There was an immediate stiffening of the limbs, a strong jerk of the head, and a piercing *"AAAAHHHHHHH!"* was emitted at high volume.

It is assumed that the subject did not suffer a heart attack, because there was still enough life left in him to attempt to strangle the researcher, and to threaten to wreck her Poolside Paradise Lego set, which she got for Christmas.

I was unable to offer Spencer much sympathy after this ordeal. As far as I'm concerned, he had it coming.

The other day I heard the front door open at about the time I expected him and Paige to arrive home from school. So I called out: "Is that you guys?"

There was no response. It seemed strange to hear the door open, but have no one answer when you called out.

So I left the kitchen and came around by the stairs, heading for the front hall.

"*BOOOOO!*"

Spencer had pressed himself up against the wall around the corner, barely breathing. The shouting of "*BOOOOO!*" was accompanied by the traditional menacing hands gesture, with the fingers stretched out à la Dracula.

This could have been the basis for another research experiment: how high can a father come off the floor without the use of cables?

Answer: higher than you might think.

Spencer's attempts to scare members of his family have taken other forms. Before the simple just-jump-out-and-scare-you routine (an old trick, but still effective), there was the almost daily appearance of the black plastic spider. One day it would be under the covers, the next day in your drink.

We'd gone grocery shopping, and the kids had settled into the backseat, each with a little bag of candies.

Said Spencer to Neetha: "Mom, there's something wrong with your makeup. It's all smudged or something. You better check it in the mirror."

He pointed to the mirror on her windshield visor, which has a little flap you have to open.

You do not need to be Miss Marple to view this suspiciously. Never in his entire life has Spencer noticed when Neetha used a new eye shadow, tried new lipstick, wore different earrings or a new scarf.

In other words, he's just like his father.

So for him to suddenly spot a makeup flaw, especially one that required Neetha to *open the little visor flap*, well, let's just say the perfect crime so far seems beyond his grasp.

"It's fine," Neetha said.

"Mom, you REALLY should check."

"Why don't you return the cart and get our quarter back?"

Spencer leapt from the car. Any trick, even one this brilliantly executed, is worth putting on hold when money is involved.

Neetha opened the flap, removed the plastic spider, and put it into his bag of candy. All in full view of Paige, who wasn't about to say a word. Spencer returned and went on about the makeup again.

"Just eat your candy and stop worrying about it," Neetha said.

We weren't quite out of the parking lot when the scream came.

No heart attack, but close.

Our new sitter is very demanding

Neetha and I were kicked out of our own house again the other night.

"Can't you guys go to a movie or the mall or something?" Spencer asked. "Go to one movie tonight, and another tomorrow night. You HAVE to go out."

"I'm tired," Neetha said. "And the last thing I want to do is drag around a mall."

"There's no decent movies playing that we haven't already seen," I said.

"But you've GOT to go out," Spencer pleaded. "I need money for the big toy show on the weekend. I'm DESPERATE for some babysitting cash."

Ever since Spencer turned twelve and graduated from the babysitting course, he's been shoving us out the front door so he can look after Paige. We've been breaking him in gently, letting him handle short jobs where we're close by. A matinee at the nearby cinema. A dinner at the neighbours' across the street.

But he wants more work. He is, after all, a guy with expenses. *Star*

Wars figures, *X-Files* trading cards. Hobby paints.

The St. John Ambulance babysitting course promised to stress such things as supervisory skills, what to do if there's an emergency, how to call 911 and communicate a problem swiftly and calmly.

But I can't help but believe someone from the Canadian Auto Workers wasn't brought in as a guest speaker. Spencer learned plenty about not opening the door to strangers, but he's also acquired these terrific new skills at negotiating.

"How much, exactly," he immediately wanted to know upon seeking his first contract, "am I going to be paid an hour?"

We made him an offer. He rejected it and put his own demands on the table. "Ha!" we laughed. "These are tough times. Don't you read the paper?" We made him a final offer. Again, a rejection, followed by a revised demand. So we made him a final, *final* offer.

After settling the dental plan issue, we reached a deal. But there was still trouble. Where was the fairness, his sister wanted to know, in Spencer being paid to stay home, without parents, while she got zip?

This involved some explanation of the concept of babysitting, that it is usually just the babysitter, and not the person being sat, who pockets the loot. But Paige still felt that if she had to endure having her own brother put in charge of her, there had to be some kind of pain and suffering allowance.

One night, Paige showed that she's really been paying attention to our advice that she speak up for herself, be a wise consumer. There was a letter addressed to us: "Dear Mom and Dad: I am not happy with this babysitter," it began.

So anyway, back to the beginning. Here we were, with a sitter, but no ambition to go out. Neetha was fighting a cold. I was just plain tired. How many times in the last twelve years would we have killed for a sitter? And now that we had one, all we wanted to do was watch *Seinfeld*.

But we called up Bob and Pat, told them we were being ordered out, and asked if they'd like to meet for coffee. They said sure. (If you measure friendship by how willing people are to be used for trivial purposes, Bob and Pat are right up there.)

As we drank our decafs, Neetha stared off into space in a new variation on sleepwalking: sleepsipping. I yawned and looked at my watch. Bob and Pat seemed to take no offence.

"Can we go home now?" I asked Neetha. After all, we'd been away at least twenty minutes.

After about an hour we went home. We'd have stayed out longer, but we hadn't brought our pyjamas. Needless to say, Spencer felt cheated that his job didn't last longer.

"Where you going tomorrow?" he demanded to know.

Maybe it would be easier just to raise his allowance.

The One Tuck Rule

We are going to have to start implementing the One Tuck Rule.

This hard-line approach is long overdue at our house, where Neetha and I have allowed things to get terribly out of hand.

Every night, shortly before Spencer and Paige turn off their lights and go to sleep, Neetha and I will slip in to do The Tuck.

Sometimes I'll be giving Paige her tuck while Neetha is in with Spencer giving him his. Then we'll pass each other in the hall or on the stairs on our way to dispense a tuck to the other child.

A tuck is a fairly straightforward ritual. Child snuggles under covers (especially during the winter), parent sits on edge of bed, slips arm around child for a hug, hands sliding between flannel pyjamas and bedsheets that are already warm, then parent leans in for a kiss.

It is customary to say a few words at this time. "You have a good sleep" is a favourite. "Sleep tight" and "Have sweet dreams" are also quite serviceable.

Sometimes there are last minute concerns from the tuckee about the day to come, as in: "Do you think I've studied enough for my French test tomorrow?" Or: "What happens if all the answers to my social studies homework are wrong?" Words of reassurance are given;

promises made that in the morning we can review things one last time, but not to worry, you're going to be just fine.

And the light goes out, and the tuck is done.

But now complications arise. Someone gets up to go to the bathroom. A mosquito bite that was scratched too vigorously now needs a bandage. An important note about an upcoming school trip that has been forgotten at the bottom of a backpack absolutely *has* to be signed tonight.

There is a spider on the ceiling.

So now that they've been out of bed to deal with any number of possible crises, no matter how briefly, they feel they are entitled to *another* tuck once they get back under the covers.

"Tuck me in!" comes the cry from down the hall.

"We already tucked you in!"

"But I had to get up!"

And so we make a return trip, do the snuggle, the hug, the kiss, the whole thing. It looks just like the first one, but on fast-forward.

Or there's the I-don't-remember-getting-tucked-in amnesia scam, which we fall for on a regular basis.

I'll be tucking in Paige, and she'll say, "Send Mom in."

On our bed I find a day-weary Neetha, who, if she were powered by batteries, would be unlikely to get an Energizer endorsement contract. Paige, I tell her, wants to be tucked in.

"But I already tucked her in."

"She's under the impression you didn't, so if you want any peace you better go now."

So this is why we are pondering the One Tuck Rule. You can't be too careful, you know. At a time when we're worried about conservation, we don't want to run out of tucks. You start giving them away willy-nilly and before you know it you haven't got any left. We do not want to become, dare I say it, tuckered out.

The only problem is, once you're back for a repeat tuck performance, giving your kids another kiss, slipping your arms around them under the covers for just one last hug, letting that warm, snuggly moment intoxicate you, you realize that this is one of the greatest feelings in the world.

So you see the problem. It's going to be tough, but we have to crack down.

Maybe next week.

Nightmares aren't just for kids

If one of the kids wakes up in the night with a bad dream, and wants to crawl into bed with me and Neetha, we pull out The Little Bed, or The Nightmare Bed, that's tucked under our own.

It's a piece of camping foam, a sleeping bag and a pillow, and we lay it out next to our bed. Even if they're not in bed with us, they're comforted that we're close by. This beats having kids in your bed every night for more reasons than I care to go into here.

But tonight, it's not Spencer or Paige who's awake after a nightmare. I'm the one who's come awake with a start, breathing quickly. I look at the clock, which now reads 2:14 a.m., and I'm grateful not to be sleeping anymore. I've had a major, cold sweat nightmare, a real beaut, and an intermission is welcome.

It was a dream that, in the light of day, would seem positively silly. But at night, silly is the stuff of Dali and Dr. Caligari. One becomes haunted by unthinkable family tragedies, ridiculous end-of-the-world scenarios, monsters, and pod people. This is what happens when you're still hooked on sci-fi long after you should have graduated to *Masterpiece Theatre*. Or maybe it's just too much fast food.

When kids have nightmares, you tell them not to worry. You tell them it's okay to be scared, but the dreams are only pictures that can't hurt you. It isn't real. It can't do you any harm. Everything will be fine.

You're struggling to keep your eyes open at this point. You are *desperate* to reassure, because you didn't get to bed until midnight and have to be up at six and haven't had a good sleep all week.

"But every time I close my eyes," they say, "the bad dreams come back."

Well, that's simple, you say. When you're dreaming, just go over to that monster and bop him right on the nose. Or think about something else, and get on with it, *please*, because *we are bushed*. Think of your favourite stuffed animal, think about building something neat with Lego. Think about something *nice*. And you plant a little kiss on their forehead and draw the covers up tight.

We parents are so wise. So knowing. So full of experience.

So why am I wide awake, afraid to close my eyes for fear the nightmare will resume like a video that's just been on pause?

Why don't I just think of something *nice*? Put some pretty pictures in *my* head? Funny how the darkness brings into focus the inadequacy of our own words of so-called wisdom.

And then I hear footsteps. Paige, in her nightie and clutching a blanket, appears in the doorway. Bad dreams are evidently going around. Again, maybe it was the onion rings.

I reach under my bed with one arm and slide out The Nightmare Bed. "Bad dream?" I ask her.

"Yes," she says quietly, tucking into the sleeping bag on the floor. I watch a while, reach down and stroke this beautiful child's face, and gently pat her hair until she seems asleep.

But in a few minutes, Paige sits up with a start. She clasps her small hands together and holds them to her chest, which is going in and out rapidly. Even though she's only a couple of feet away from me, she looks all alone in the darkness, so frightened, caught in the glow of the streetlights coming in through the blinds and the numbers of the clock that now read 2:37 a.m.

"What is it, honey?" I whisper. "The bad dream again?"

She nods. I pull back the covers and pat the sheet. "Come on." She crawls in with me and Neetha and plops her head down on my pillow, leaving me to struggle to find a few square inches to lay my noggin back down.

Finally, she's in a restful sleep. And I can no longer keep my eyes open. But how bad can a nightmare be now, I think, with Paige here at my side to protect me.

Where the Heart Is

It's almost bedtime, and Spencer and I are goofing around with the model railway we've been constructing in the basement furnace room, off and on, for the last few months.

"Goofing" would certainly seem to be the operative word, at least where I'm concerned. I'm the only person I know to have caused a major derailment with his nose. It happened while trying to get a close-up view of a train going by, one squinted eye poised over the boxcars as they passed.

This went fine until the end of the train arrived, and the cupola, that part of the caboose that has windows and sits on top, caught my nose, knocking the caboose off the track and pulling the rest of the train off with it. Not the sort of thing you want to mention on your resume if you're applying for a job at CN.

Anyway, despite the occasional goofing around, Spencer and I are having a sort of serious chat. What will happen with this railway, Spencer wants to know, years from now, when I become decrepit and am drooling into my coffee, can no longer take care of myself and must be admitted to some kind of home? You know, like when I'm fifty?

Well, I say, it will probably become his responsibility. He may have a family of his own by the time I've reached that state, and if he still wants the railway he'll have to dismantle it, pack it up, and take it to his place.

Would it be possible, he wants to know, to make a hole in the base-ment ceiling and have the whole thing lifted out in one piece through the living room? No, I say, that would be a bit impractical.

And before we know it, this turns into a discussion of how I had to sort through things that belonged to my parents after they each died, and how that's one of the unpleasant responsibilities that eventually befall children. And we realize that we are talking now about something much more than what to do with a few engines and tracks and miniature buildings.

I tell him to get ready for bed, and that after I've been up to see what his sister's up to, Neetha and I will drop around later to say goodnight.

I wander up the steps of this place that is our home, finding the kitchen nearly dark but for one fluorescent tube over the counter and the lights from the front step casting shadows through the door and into the hall. I climb another flight and find Paige already tucked under the covers, clutching her stuffed dog Muttsy and awaiting her kiss.

She asks her nightly question: "What should I think about?" She likes to have a little scenario to imagine. It helps her get to sleep. Imagine you are in *Cats*, I say. Or that you are flying over the countryside like a bird. Or maybe you're a secret agent on a dangerous mission.

It's a challenge coming up with something different every night. Some nights I am Lazy Dad. I cop out. "Just go to sleep," I say.

But we finally come up with something ("How would the world be different if it were run by dogs?") and I give her a kiss, and I give Muttsy a kiss, too. I slip out the door and move down the hall into our bedroom and talk with Neetha for a while.

"You'll never guess how I hurt my nose," I say.

A kind of satisfying exhaustion sets in about this time. We can remember nights when, before kids, our evening *began* at 9 p.m. Now we hope we'll be awake when Peter Mansbridge reads the evening's headlines. But we're not complaining. Life under this roof is good.

Before long we realize it's time Spencer turned his light out. I head back downstairs to check on him. "Tell Spence I'll be down in a minute to say goodnight," Neetha says.

He's sitting up in bed, the light on next to him, his drawing pad in his lap. He has been sketching a superhero with incredible biceps.

Spencer says he's been thinking a lot about our earlier talk.

He says: "I want things to stay the same. I want things in our house to always be the way they are right now."

What do you know, I say. Dads feel that way sometimes, too.

Acknowledgements

Thanks to John Honderich and Lou Clancy of *The Toronto Star* for giving me the chance to return to writing, thereby preventing the kind of damage I could have done in management, and for allowing me to use material here that originally appeared in the *Star*. To Steve Nease, thanks again for providing cartoons that convey in an instant what it takes me 600 words to get across. To our friends Bob and Pat Richardson, whose misadventures I have misappropriated as though they were our own, you have my gratitude and apologies. And I remain grateful for the support of Stoddart's Don Bastian, and editor Marnie Kramarich, whose vision for organizing this book has convinced me to have her put an addition on our house.

Finally, to Neetha, Spencer, and Paige, where would I be without you guys?